Enhancing

Emotional Intelligence

BOOKS BY THESE AUTHORS

Enhancing Emotional Intelligence

Managing Change with Personal Resilience

Mastering Team Leadership

The Team Training Manual

The Adventures of a Self-Managing Team

Enhancing

Emotional Intelligence

Leadership Tips from the Executive Coach

Robert Ferguson, PhD
&
Mark Kelly, MBA

Mark Kelly Books
Raleigh, North Carolina

Book orders: For single copies, order from Amazon.com.
For quantity discounts and special arrangements, call Mark Kelly
at (919) 783-7660

Learn more about executive coaching, leadership development,
training and workshops, or speaking to groups.

Visit our website at RaleighConsulting.com

This book is dedicated to our parents.

Harvey & Marilyn

Helen & Jim

CONTENTS

PREFACE

We have worked with many leaders over the years. Some were quite deficient at competencies of emotional intelligence and needed a kind of "basic training" approach to working effectively with people. Most were competent at several aspects of emotional intelligence and wanted to improve on or expand their strengths in response to new challenges. All were eager to improve their leadership abilities. We are grateful to all of the supervisors, managers, and executives with whom we have worked, as we have had the good fortune to learn and grow from others even as we helped them learn and grow.

We are also grateful to the many researchers in emotional intelligence. This book does not offer any new research, but rather attempts to put into the most readable and practical form results from recent years of investigation into what makes individuals, teams, and organizations succeed. A special note of thanks goes to author Daniel Goleman, whose books and articles have helped make the subject of emotional intelligence more widely known and understood.

We are also profoundly grateful to colleagues and mentors who encouraged us to write this book, and who provided candid feedback. Our gratitude also goes to the many people who gave us permission to tell their stories. We use pseudonyms, but the stories are true.

Finally, we would like to express our gratitude to family members who patiently put up with our meetings, our writing time, and our obsession with the topics of emotional intelligence and leadership.

Getting The Biggest Bang For Your Buck From This Book

You don't need to read this entire book. We wrote it for busy people who want to grow without obsessing. Think of it as a desk reference; pull it off the shelf when and where there's a need. Think of it as a web site; "click" for byte-size strategies you can use right away. Think of it as a tool-box; grab only what the job calls for.

Write in it. Tear out pages. Leave it in the restroom for brief study sessions. Put it in a brown paper bag and give it to your boss (anonymously).

If you _are_ the boss, use it to prepare performance evaluations. Use it to coach others. Use it to coach yourself.

Most of all: use it to grow and help others grow. But get specific with what you want to change. Build on your strengths. Don't try to change too much too fast. And don't push others too fast or they won't change at all.

Once you zoom in on a competency you want to enhance, practice the behaviors again and again. Don't perfect it; just get good at it. Get more comfortable with it. If you're coaching others, DO NOT insist on mastery. When someone gets pretty good at something, they'll have a million opportunities to practice it in the coming years.

Leadership develops over a lifetime.

Overview of Emotional Intelligence: Leadership, Your Career, Your Organization

Leaders lead people. That's true whether . . .

- you have management responsibilities in a company
- you work in educational leadership
- you influence a non-profit
- you share leadership of a small team
- you are an entrepreneur or business owner
- you are an independent professional (attorney, accountant, physician, etc.).

Whatever the size or goals of your organization, you can't lead technology or numbers or strategic plans. You can only lead *people*. It's people who will implement your plans, sell your products, and provide service to your clientele.

Some of those people will be inspired and highly competent. They will be easy to lead. Others will be difficult, or inexperienced, or resistant to change, or irritable. They'll be a challenge to lead.

Among your jobs as a leader is to build teams and mentor other leaders. Your work is bigger than you are. It requires collaboration, and it requires other people with leadership abilities to build upon your contributions.

Leadership and teamwork all require emotional intelligence. Your career and your organization will thrive to the extent that you recruit and develop people with this set of competencies.

What is emotional intelligence?[1] It is a set of competencies for effectively managing our relationships and ourselves. Whereas traditional notions of intelligence refer to intellectual abilities, emotional intelligence refers to "a different way of being smart."[2] The specific skills that comprise emotional intelligence have to do with self-knowledge, ability to read individuals and groups, and the ability to communicate with and influence others. People who are "smart" in these ways tend to be very effective in their personal relationships as well as business interactions, organizational challenges, collaboration, and leadership. An abundance of research has established that higher levels of emotional intelligence lead to more productive and innovative teams, better retention of talent, more resilience in the face of organizational change, and the economic benefits that come from all of the above.[3]

What are the four dimensions of emotional intelligence?[4]

♦ **Self-Awareness:** the ability to monitor one's own emotions, thoughts, and behaviors, accurately assess one's strengths and weaknesses, and maintain a high level of self-worth and respect.

♦ **Self-Management:** the ability to adapt to change, regulate one's emotions according to the situation, take effective actions toward goals, reach for self-improvement, act with integrity, act on opportunities, and see the glass as half full rather than half empty.

♦ **People Radar:** the ability to understand others, recognize and attend to customer's needs, and sense the political relationships and culture within an organization.

♦ **People Skills:** the ability to inspire, mentor, initiate change, work effectively through conflicts, influence and motivate others, and collaborate.

What do these competencies have to do with work and leadership?

If you have management responsibilities in a large company: American companies are changing. They used to create wealth and jobs through manufacturing—they used to mostly *make* things. Now they mostly invent things, assemble things, or provide services. Companies that *invent* things need people with emotional intelligence because inventions are complex. It takes collaboration and leadership to develop new technology. Today's innovations are far too complex for solo efforts. Today's innovations take a team of sharp minds working symbiotically. Companies that *assemble* things are probably dealing with suppliers all over the world. Interacting effectively with people from other cultures requires a higher level of people skills. Companies that mostly provide *services* are in the business of making people feel satisfied when experiencing a need or a problem. That takes awareness, service orientation, collaboration, communications skills, and other competencies. There are many companies outside the United States that can offer cheaper labor, high-tech capabilities, and proximity to more rapidly expanding markets. The United States economy depends on workers and leaders with emotional intelligence to compete worldwide.

If you work in educational leadership: In the private school world, the parents of your students are customers. In the public school world, the parents are constituents. Either way, you have to please and impress them to consider your school a success. You have to work effectively with parents, students, staff, the board, and sometimes the press. How

well you manage your emotions and these many relationships determines how well you and other educational leaders manage your school.

If you influence a non-profit: You need to convince
people to give money, *and* you have to get people to do noble things with fewer resources and less pay than they could
make in the profit sector. That two-fold purpose demands
exquisite communication and relationships skills, as well as
a crystal clear sense of purpose.

If you share leadership of a small team: A group of
people with plenty of technical knowledge may or may not
accomplish much. But teams with adequate technical
knowledge that are also characterized by a wealth of emotional intelligence tend to be more innovative, motivated,
flexible, resilient, and focused. They handle setbacks better.
They allow for conflict and use it to their advantage. They
solve problems and move on. The team leader who has an
opportunity to recruit partly based on these competencies is
setting him or herself up for team success. The same team
leader who leads in such way as to enhance the emotional
intelligence of the team is going even further to ensure success.[5]

If you are an entrepreneur or business owner: Your
gift is to bring an idea to reality. But you can't do it your-

self. You need to lead others who contribute to the realization of your dream. Many entrepreneurs and business owners intimidate and threaten the very people who are necessary for helping them succeed. Doesn't make sense, does it? Most successful entrepreneurs are talented not only at seeing business opportunities and understanding the market—they also have a way with people. They inspire others to cooperate, to work hard, and to engage effectively with customers. Success requires technical knowledge, business knowledge, and people knowledge.

If you are an independent professional (attorney, accountant, physician, etc.): You provide a service to people who can buy the same service down the street. Unless you are the only local genius in your field, it's the relationships you build that will determine the quality and quantity of your work. It is also your emotional intelligence that will influence how much of a leader you can become in your community. Community leadership requires people radar, initiative, communication skills, and more. These are all things they probably do not teach in graduate school, law school, or medical training.

Can someone learn emotional intelligence? Yes. Most people are already adept at one or more emotional intelligence skills. And most people can enhance their current abilities as well as make improvements in areas where they are underdeveloped. Which skills to improve depend on the nature of the job and the overall climate of the organization. It is not necessary to be highly skilled at all aspects of emotional intelligence.

But enhancing emotional intelligence is best accomplished with certain help and methods. This book emphasizes pragmatic and proven techniques for helping you enhance these competencies.

Can you hire for emotional intelligence? Yes. And you should. Today's technical skills are best thought of as threshold skills. They get you in the door. If you are an engineer, you need plenty of engineering knowledge. But as projects require collaboration and leadership skills, your engineering knowledge will be less and less relevant. Selecting people with emotional intelligence competencies—and who also have a willingness to further enhance their emotional intelligence—increases the probability of getting the job done.

What are the benefits to the individual of enhancing emotional intelligence?[6] Research indicates the following benefits:

♦ Career advancement
♦ Increased, more sustainable productivity

- More effective management skills
- Better ways of dealing with stress
- Higher level of career satisfaction
- Fewer unnecessary conflicts
- More collegial relationships
- Lower probability of derailing career through disruptive emotions

What are the benefits to the organization?[7]

- Economic benefits (higher sales, revenues, profits)
- Better ability to compete in global economy driven by innovation, service-orientation, information management, and rapid change
- Better ability to leverage diversity
- Higher productivity, especially in complex jobs
- Better ability to make productive use of highly intelligent workers
- Lower turnover
- Better hiring decisions
- Fewer formal grievances by employees
- Fewer lost-time accidents
- More effective management
- Workers are more likely to communicate with managers with higher levels of emotional intelligence

♦   Better communication among managers

How do you develop emotional intelligence in yourself and others? While it is very possible to enhance your own emotional intelligence, or to help someone else do so, it takes a plan and it takes a method. Change, especially *sustainable* change, is more than a fad or a single technique. If you want to grow as a leader and get better results, you have to invest time and motivation. And you have to approach your development goals methodically and repeatedly.

You may decide to work with a coach, either in a formal sense by hiring an executive coach, or informally by asking a colleague to help you set and work toward goals. You also have to break down the competency into its parts.

What is a competency? We have broken down each competency of emotional intelligence into the four areas below.

♦   **ATTITUDES:** Emotionally charged beliefs about what is important, and an overall mental framework about the competency. We have included examples of attitudes that support each competency.

♦   **ACTIONS:** *Skills* and *behaviors* that let you practice some specific part of that competency. We have in-

cluded many pragmatic suggestions to help you or
someone else develop specific skills.

♦ **LANGUAGE:** How to verbally communicate to others
that you are competent in this area. For each competency, several examples of effective language are provided.

♦ **SELF-TALK:** Self-talk is the private discussion we
have with ourselves in our minds. Everyone engages in
self-talk throughout the day. You can intentionally direct your self-talk toward a specific skill or behavior,
such as staying calm, asserting yourself, showing empathy, etc. Leadership ultimately begins with how you
lead yourself. And you lead yourself, in part, through
the thoughts you choose to think. For each leadership
competency, several examples of relevant self-talk are
included.

We need competent leaders at all levels of society: the
kid on the playground who puts together the kickball team,
to the neighborhood activist, to the professional contributing
to his or her community, to the corporate executive, to the
government official. Leaders, as we said at the beginning,
lead people. Our mission is to help you lead people effectively so you and your team can accomplish important goals

and make this world a better place. The mission of this book is to make these leadership skills clear, practical and most of all—*practicable*.

Part One:
Self-Awareness

1. Focus Your Internal Observatory

Emotional self-awareness:
Monitoring your thoughts and emotions,
and realizing their effect on your behavior,
your job performance, and on others.

"What you are aware of you are in control of;
what you are not aware of is in control of you."
—Anthony de Mello

"My company is small," explains Dan. "But some of the companies I supply are very big." He designs special machines for advanced manufacturing.

Over the years he has discovered the business value of emotional awareness.

"I really don't deal with companies. I deal with individuals. Someone who can describe what a project needs and decide if I can do it.

"I remember dealing with an overconfident lead engineer from one of the big car companies. He was telling his team why my machine wouldn't do what they needed. But his facts were wrong; he was jumping to conclusions. I started feeling hot. My throat was tight. I felt insulted, angry. I was about to lose a huge contract because of this guy's ego. But I knew if I went with my feelings I'd say something I'd regret. When I get stressed like that, I can stop listening and get preachy. I make people defensive.

"So I made myself relax. I loosened up my shoulders. I relaxed my face. I listened. I asked questions. Without openly disagreeing with the guy, I got him to think through his problem and reconsider his assumptions. Finally he changed his mind about my machine. But I let him keep his big ego. I didn't take him head on. I stayed aware of my emotions and kept them in check. And I got the job."

Emotional Self-Awareness

Awareness is the first building block for all people skills. You can't make decisions or forge relationships without using your senses and your mind to observe the inner world *and* the outer world. It's the foundation for all effective communication and collaboration. It's a necessary prerequisite for emotional control, empathy, customer service, measured responses during tense situations, and the ability to inspire or persuade others. It's one of the foundations of great leadership.

ATTITUDES

- Self-awareness is not merely a "touchy-feely" nicety.
- Self-awareness is practical.
- Self-awareness is a prerequisite for important organizational skills.
- Self-awareness supports a good decision-making process.
- Leadership involves awareness of thoughts and emotions, and knowing how they affect behavior.
- The higher the stakes, the more important this competency becomes.

ACTIONS

Focus by choice. You can "point" your awareness, as if it's a flashlight. Within a few moments you can consciously seek data from your mental and emotional world—data that can have an impact on how effective you are in what you say and how you interact with others. You can also direct the flashlight of your awareness outward. You can focus on a particular person to notice subtle signals of positive or negative emotion. Focusing carefully on someone else at just the right moment can influence what to say (or not say) in sales, leadership, and team situations.

Stop other activity to reflect inward. To focus by choice, it's best to take a short break from other activities. For example, prior to an important meeting, spend three to five uninterrupted minutes doing some of the tips below. Investing this small amount of time once or twice a day will have substantial payback.

Silently ask yourself about yourself. Search inward for information about emotion, intentions, desires, needs, thought patterns, and motivation. By doing this you will empower yourself to communicate well, manage frustration, and stay focused. Sometimes we know instantly what we want from an interaction with someone; other times we need to reflect and clarify, which can take some time.

Observe your thoughts. What images are you holding in your mind? What are you saying to yourself about the upcoming situation? Are you ruminating about something?

Your thoughts, especially thoughts that occur in patterns, influence your behavior. Being aware of your thought patterns, including unpleasant ones, is an important step toward addressing problems and worries so they do not subconsciously sabotage your effectiveness.

Observe physical clues. Sense whether any part of your body is tense. Is there an ache or a pain that is affecting you emotionally? Or do you feel energetic, strong, relaxed? When you cannot detect clear direct information as to your state of mind, physical clues can tell you. If you don't feel angry, but you notice you're clenching your fists under the table or grinding your teeth, maybe your body is trying to tell you something.

Review recent statements and behaviors. Think back on the last few days. Notice any patterns? Have you been mostly optimistic and engaged with others? Or do you notice that you've been moody or impatient? Sometimes our pattern of behavior tells us more about our emotions than directly looking inward.

Notice indirect feedback. Think back to recent comments and reactions of others. People are always giving informal feedback to each other, such as a smile or a compliment on the one hand, or a scowl or complaint on the other. What are people informally telling you about your mood and behavior? EXAMPLES: "You seem preoccupied." Or "I can tell you're feeling better about the project lately."

Seek direct feedback. It's good to have some relationships in which you can candidly ask for feedback about your emotions and behavior. EXAMPLES: "How did I come off in that meeting this morning?" Or "Do I seem moody lately?"

Talk to a good listener. Sometimes it's easier to become aware of what you are thinking and feeling through conversation. Someone who listens well can help you bring out subtleties of mood and thought so you can act on them more consciously and effectively. You can start such a conversation like this: "I'd like to talk through something with you. You're a good listener and it helps me sort out what I'm thinking."

Write. In a journal or on a computer, recording your thoughts, impressions and reactions to events helps you become more aware. On a computer you can easily search for key words in your journal, making it easy to refer back to other times you experienced anger, or nervousness, or thought a particular thought. This ability to refer back to similar moments of awareness lets you see patterns. Awareness of your patterns of thoughts, emotions and behaviors is the main building block to understanding yourself.

Ask someone to observe your "audience." Whether you are running a meeting or addressing a group of people, you are having an effect on the people around you. Do you know what that effect is? It is difficult to observe everything when there are a number of people in the room. You can scan the room from time to time to try to be aware of how others are reacting to you, but you will miss something. Asking a trusted colleague to observe how others respond to you—and to have that colleague share his or her observations with you later—provides valuable information about your effect on others.

Ask about others' awareness. Ask someone what he or she observes about you. If you ask the right person, you'll learn something valuable about yourself. If the person is observant and candid, you might learn that you look nervous at the beginning of a speech when you thought you looked relaxed. You might learn that you *don't* look nervous when indeed you felt so. You might learn that what you thought came across as funny actually appeared flippant or insensitive. To fine tune your awareness of yourself, ask others to tell you what they see and hear.

Use audio or video recordings. To be more aware of how you come across in a speech or a meeting, you can literally study yourself from another perspective by taping yourself. This is easiest and least obtrusive with audio, of course. You'll notice things about your behavior, intonation, rapport with the group, etc., that you might never know from your own point of view.

LANGUAGE

- "I need some time to reflect on my reactions to the meeting."
- "Let me think about that and get back to you."
- "I'm uncomfortable with this new approach, but I can't quite put my finger on what's bothering me. Let me consider what we've talked about and respond later."
- "I wonder what you noticed about me when I was addressing the group."
- "Would you be willing to take some notes in the meeting? I'd like to get a sense of how others react to my leadership style. "

SELF-TALK

- *What is happening inside of me?*
- *What am I thinking or feeling about this situation?*
- *What cues can I observe about the emotion and state of mind of people around me?*
- *What do I want from this situation?*
- *Is this emotion part of a pattern?*
- *How am I coming across to this group?*

2. Polish the Inner Mirror

Accurate self-assessment:
Candidly and realistically evaluating your
strengths and limitations, welcoming feedback,
and showing a willingness to ask for help.

"Knowing others is intelligence;
knowing yourself is true wisdom."
—Lao Tzu

Suzanne is a strong leader because she emphasizes her strengths and admits her weaknesses. With people approaching her constantly, she is in frequent conversation and must generate a lot of written communication.

When producing formal writing, she asks others for feedback by handing someone a draft along with a red pen and saying, "Writing is not my strength; please tell me how to improve this letter."

When someone comments on her email grammar or spelling, she replies, "I'm really not a writer. I'd rather discuss this, but today's schedule is tight. Please consider my email as an informal way of sharing an idea. Let's talk when we can."

Because she doesn't shy away from the inner mirror, she is known for having candor and humor about her limitations. This makes her approachable, and fosters trust and creditability. She doesn't pay too high a price in morale when she makes unpopular decisions or asks people to change. And she doesn't intimidate others (or stress herself) with perfectionism.

Enhancing Accurate Self-Assessment

An open system is more likely to grow and adapt than is a closed system. This is true of governments, organizations, teams, and individuals. When you can see yourself through another's eyes, you can be more honest and accurate about how you help or hinder progress. An absence of this competency results in extreme insecurity or arrogance, poor judgment, and thus poor leadership. Fine-tuning your ability to assess your strengths and limitations leads to higher quality work, professional growth, better contributions to organizations, and ultimately to wisdom.

ATTITUDES

♦ Every strength is a weakness; every weakness is strength—it depends on the situation.

♦ Leadership is not about being good at everything; it's about leveraging my strengths and those of others.

♦ We need teams and organizations because a diverse group is more talented than an individual.

♦ Continuous improvement is not the same as perfectionism.

ACTIONS

Ask several people to list three of your strengths and three of your limitations.[8] Select certain people who don't have an overly developed need to please. You want a candid, balanced view. This can be done in a candid conversation, or by email. First, have a candid conversation, telling them what you're trying to do and why it is important to you. Second, stress your desire for *three* examples of strengths and limitations. This pushes them to go beyond the first thought. Third, thank them for whatever they say, whether you like hearing it or not, and whether or not you agree. You are thanking them for their perspective. You have time to judge the accuracy of their feedback. Be sure to ask several people, if possible, so you can see patterns. If more than one person identifies something as a strength or a weakness, it is more likely to be true.

Prompt for feedback. When you want someone's feedback, start with general prompts; follow up with specific prompts. General prompts: "I'd like to hear any feedback you have about my speech." Or, "Be honest with me about what I did well and not-so-well on that conference call." Specific prompts: "Do you think my speech was too long?" Or, "You thought it was effective that I opened the meeting with humor and put people at ease. That's helpful to know. I'd like to also hear what parts of the meeting I didn't handle so well."

Affirm & prompt again. Affirm: Reward the person giving you feedback, even if you disagree or it bothers you.

The feedback may be accurate or not, painful or not, valuable or not. But every time you get feedback and reward the person giving it to you, it's an investment in a feedback relationship. Prompt again. If the first time you ask for feedback you get a vague "you're fine," politely ask for more. People have to believe you want real feedback, and not just bland praise. The other person probably thinks you don't really want feedback, and so you probably will have to prompt and re-prompt to convince others that you really *really* want to know how they perceive you.

Review comments about your strengths. Make a list of the kinds of positive comments you've heard about yourself inside and outside of work. If there are patterns, there is probably some truth to it even if some of it sounds like flattery.

Review comments about your limitations. Make a list of the kinds of complaints or criticisms you've heard about yourself inside and outside of work. If there are patterns, there is probably some truth to it even if it stings or you think the comments are exaggerated.

The Sandwich Technique: Do this for others and they will do it for you. Offer an affirming comment, followed by a suggestion for improvement, followed by another affirming comment. The other person still gets to feel good about his or herself, but they also hear the message about limitations. You will be helping someone else develop more accurate self-assessment, and they are more likely to do the same for you.

Write about the year (or decade) in review. Pick a timeframe and write down your accomplishments and setbacks. Analyze them for evidence of what you tend to do well, and where you tend to stumble or run into your limitations. Then share this writing with a trusted friend, colleague, mentor or coach for further discussion and clarification for a thorough self-assessment.

Push others for in-depth performance appraisals. Managers usually don't tell the whole truth when evaluating others. If you ask specific questions and make it clear you really want to know how you can improve, you're more likely to get practical information.

Respond as feedback is given. Avoid defensiveness or explaining. Take in the feedback and ask only clarifying questions that do not discourage further feedback.

Ask for help. Here's how: "You're very good at details and numbers; would you help me by reviewing my report and telling me how I can improve it?"

Don't shoot the messenger. Practice good listening and emotional control when someone is giving feedback.

Take time to evaluate negative feedback and ask for another perspective from someone who is not going to automatically take your side. It takes patience to evaluate feedback that is unpleasant. You may ultimately disagree with it, but to do so too quickly may prevent you from getting value out of an otherwise unpleasant source of information. Separate the style of the message from the content. You may have a colleague with terrible communication skills who nonetheless has valuable points. If you feel harshly criticized, discuss the criticism with someone wise and objective.

Participate in assessment techniques and coaching. Professional coaches are trained to help people learn accurate self-assessment. The tools of their trade include 360° feedback, personality assessments, and interviewing. You can then learn about your personality type to better understand about what strengths and limitations tend to be associated with your type.

Take time away from the job or project to calmly take a clear look at yourself. We tend to get defensive during busy, stressful times at work. Stepping back from the situation, literally and figuratively, might give you the sense of safety you need to really consider what you do well and where you tend to perform less effectively.

Create strong relationships that offer an ongoing feedback loop. In the long run, strong personal and professional relationships that offer ongoing feedback give powerful and pragmatic benefits to your leadership development.

LANGUAGE

- "I'd like your perspective on how I handled a situation."
- "Would you be willing to give me candid feedback?"
- "I'm trying to get a clear view of my leadership style. Would you be willing to tell me what you see as my leadership strengths, as well as where I could be more effective?"
- "Since you worked with me on the project, would you tell me what you saw as my strengths and weaknesses?"
- "Thanks, that is really helpful feedback. I'm going to think about everything you said."

SELF-TALK

- *I don't have to be perfect; I just have to find the right match between my skills and the needs of the group.*
- *I can emphasize my strengths and delegate or otherwise compensate for my weakness.*
- *I will ultimately be more effective and successful as a leader if I am realistic about my abilities.*

3. Refuel Your Personal Power Source

Self-confidence:
The ability to sense your self worth,
be empowered by self-respect,
and emphasize your strengths.

"Nothing can be done without
hope and confidence."
—Helen Keller

"I was good at sales, but struggled with confidence in the early years." Julie loved the real estate business, yet hated showing properties.

When she started managing other salespeople, Julie's confidence grew. "I think it's because I liked my work more; I have more of a natural talent for managing than for selling." But she eventually tired of working for someone else. "So I started building my own business. I realize now that I was building my self-confidence, too."

Eventually Julie became quite prosperous, and *very* confident in her work. "Work was my main source of pride. It was in my personal life that I lived with self-doubt."

So she worked harder. She became even more confident in her work. And her life got so out of balance she started to burn out.

"I lost the confidence I had become addicted to." She had to learn how to refuel her personal power source.

"Now I get my confidence from several sources. At work, I'm more realistic about what I'm good at and what I'm not. I hire people for the tasks that erode my confidence. I also make sure I get away from work. I play with my grandchildren. I have a relationship with God."

Julie's confidence shows in her combination of satisfaction and success.

—31—

Enhancing Self-Confidence

Organizational life contains elements of cooperation and competition. Both require self-confidence. When you are cooperating, you need to compromise, negotiate, manage conflict, and work with people of different cultures and personalities. When you are competing, you have to take risks, get your ego bruised, and celebrate success without conceit. Self-confidence makes it possible to do all of these things. A lack of self-confidence leads to excessive anxiety, and easily hurt feelings. A lack of self-confidence can also appear as arrogance (a camouflage for feelings of inferiority). Self-confidence also contributes to resilience when things go wrong or stress mounts.

ATTITUDES

♦ In order to be effective and successful, it helps to think and act with confidence.

♦ Confidence is not about faking or denying your limitations.

♦ Self-confidence is based on accurate self-assessment and playing on strengths.

♦ If you continue to develop your skills, your confidence will grow and remain strong.

♦ Self-confidence is different from arrogance.

♦ Competence feeds confidence.

ACTIONS

Practice self-confident thoughts and self-talk. We lead with our thoughts. One important aspect of confidence is how you think and what you silently say to yourself. If you repeatedly remind yourself about your mistakes and failures, you will be whittling away at confidence. If you only remind yourself about your successes, you might become overconfident and take unwise risks. We all talk to ourselves in our minds. Confident people remind themselves of their successes and setbacks and keep things in perspective.

Keep an up-to-date résumé. Your résumé is a chance to brag to the job market. As such, it also builds confidence. Even if you don't show it to other potential employers for years at a time, you'll be bolstering your confidence with a record of your accomplishments. It can also hurt your confidence to stay in a job that is toxic or a dead end. Keeping your résumé up-to-date reminds you that you can leave if you have to.

Make a list of your unofficial accomplishments that you can't include on your résumé. In addition to this or that job-well-done, list what you have done well in the last year. Include non-career items (e.g. helped a friend in need, was supportive to my spouse, built a tree house, etc.) Confidence is partly about being a good professional, and partly about being a good, loving person who contributes to others' happiness.

Rehearse. When preparing for a speech, a meeting, or an important discussion with a colleague, don't wing it. Do the appropriate amount of preparation and you'll go into the situation feeling ready and "on your toes." That builds self-confidence.

Don't apologize for stating your opinion. The point isn't whether you are right or wrong. All of us are right sometimes, and wrong other times. The point is that you have something to contribute to a discussion. Remind yourself frequently that you have something of value to give.

Practice non-verbal behaviors that illustrate confidence. When you project confidence, people respond to you in ways that help maintain and increase your self-confidence. Non-verbal confident behaviors include: upright posture, relaxed movements, frequent eye contact, assertive but warm tone of voice, and appropriate facial expression.

Cultivate friendship and work relationships with people who build your confidence. This doesn't mean these people never give you negative feedback. But it means you have several people in your corner who know the real you and are invested in your having a positive view of yourself.

Make a list of your values and dreams. Confidence is not just about what you've done, it is also about what you stand for and where you're going.

Keep learning; keep practicing. Life is long. And there is an infinite number of ways to learn. Learning and confidence building are about curiosity and an open mind. If you ever stop learning, you'll start to stagnate. Learn through formal channels such as taking a course. Or learn on your own through reading and self-study. Or learn through new experiences, or simply listening to others. Increasing your *competence* will increase your *confidence*.

Set achievable goals. Get help with this if necessary. Set yourself up to succeed, and then set higher goals if you want to. Create through realistic goal setting the positive feelings and confidence that come with crossing the finish line.

Promise less than you can deliver. Whenever you have an option, pause before you agree to take on more work or more responsibility. After 24 hours, you might feel differently. When you over-commit, you under-perform. That does not build self-confidence.

Ask for positive feedback. While in the long run we need feedback about our strengths and our weakness, it is good on occasion to ask for only positive feedback. Everyone needs a shot of confidence sometimes.

Catch someone doing something right. By affirming others, rewarding them, and pointing out what someone is doing right, you help create a culture in which people notice the positive and comment on it. You can help develop an atmosphere where everyone's confidence is supported.

Cultivate open mindedness. Self-confidence is not to be confused with stubbornness. You project and increase your confidence when you state your needs and opinions directly. But don't assume you are right and others are wrong. Open your mind to the perspective of others and be ready to change. Remember: all of us are smarter than any of us.

LANGUAGE

♦ "I was impressed with the way you handled that difficult client yesterday."

♦ "I think your ideas are good for the company."

♦ "I'd like to work with you on that; I think I can learn some new skills on this project."

♦ "I can take care of that for you."

♦ "Tell me what I'm doing right."

- "I could use some reassurance about how the project is going."

SELF-TALK

- *I don't have to know everything.*
- *There are several things I am very good at.*
- *I have the right to my perspective and opinions.*
- *My life and my career and my decisions belong to me.*
- *I contribute something of value to this organization.*
- *What can I learn from this that will bolster my confidence?*

Part Two:
Self-Management

4. Orchestrate Your Emotions

Self-regulation:
The capacity to manage your positive and negative emotions, control impulses, deal with stress effectively, and stay clear-minded.

" . . . your emotional awareness and abilities to handle feelings will determine your success and happiness in all walks of life . . ."
—John Gottman

As plant manager for a startup, Anthony led a group of inexperienced workers. He coached new employees as he did young soccer players, patiently teaching the basics. "We're gradually moving the ball down the field," he'd say.

But after two years his style changed. The plant produced too much waste. Production lagged. Upper management applied pressure to "move the ball down the field— *faster.*"

Anthony responded with frequent and impulsive anger. His harmonious relationships became discordant. Reports of problems were met with fury. "Why wasn't I told earlier?" he shouted.

Eventually his people saw him as out of control. Management heard about it and threatened to fire him.

A consultant helped him see how his outbursts led to people avoiding him. Anthony decided to return to basics. He was still an effective soccer coach. "I don't yell at kids. That would make problems worse."

He approached issues differently, teaching problem-solving skills. He rebuilt team relationships so that glitches got reported sooner. He identified other operations problems and addressed them.

Because he orchestrated his emotions, effectiveness gradually improved.

Enhancing Self-Regulation

Nothing derails a career like excessive or inappropriate emotion. Emotion has a place in the world of work, for sure. Without emotion, there would be no passion, no vision, no enthusiasm, and no compassion. Some people, however, need to improve their ability to control emotion. They cry or rant or worry aloud too often. They blow up. They lose credibility. Too much emotion, or ill-timed emotion, disconnects key players. If a leader is too emotional, people stop telling him or her important information. In the other direction, a person who can focus emotion is able to inspire and persuade others. Anger, if well timed and controlled, can alert people to problems or mistakes. Emotional self-regulation is extremely important and has a profound impact on the bottom line.

ATTITUDES

- Emotions are important and necessary, and need to be regulated.
- Uncontrolled expression of emotion is ineffective.
- Overly emotional people lose respect and credibility.
- Anger without good timing and reason hurts morale.

ACTIONS

Ask for feedback on your emotional style. Do you have a sounding board who can candidly tell you what others say about you? Would people say you have an anger problem, or that you are too sensitive and get upset easily?

Reason with yourself. People who have problems regulating their emotions often engage in "emotional reasoning." If Jeff has a feeling his job is threatened or that so-and-so doesn't like him, he jumps to the conclusion that it must indeed be true. This makes him *more* emotional, which may lead to a self-fulfilling prophecy. Reasoning with himself before accepting his emotional conclusions involves looking for clear evidence of what his emotions are trying to tell him. He may be assuming things that are not supported by evidence.

Reason with someone else. Jeff will be even better off if he reasons through his concerns with someone else. He may or may not conclude that his job is indeed threatened or someone doesn't like him. If his concerns *are* accurate, he can decide what the reasonable response is and thus avoid making a bad situation worse by over-reacting emotionally. Double checking your logic with a trusted advisor can help prevent emotional overreaction.

Learn how to pause. Some people go with their "gut reaction" too often. In very tense situations, "gut reactions" are less likely to be appropriate than reactions tempered by time and reflection. In meetings or work sessions that are tense or upsetting to you, learn some techniques for NOT expressing your emotions right away. Some of these techniques include:

♦ Slowly counting to twenty-five when you are aware of strong emotion.

♦ Biting your lip. This isn't a joke. You can't talk if you are applying mild pressure to your lower lip. Nobody knows what you're doing but you. You're telling yourself not to go with your gut reaction. Combine this with self-talk described below.

♦ Take a time out. In many situations you can excuse yourself from a meeting (say you need to use the restroom or make an important phone call). You can go somewhere to get a few moments of privacy and calm yourself down before returning to the situation that is evoking strong emotion.

Avoid major decisions during peaks of emotion. Lack of emotional regulation often leads to poor decisions. Few decisions need to be made immediately. Those that do rarely have to be made by one person. In any case, if you are highly anxious or angry or otherwise upset, simply defer the decision for a few hours or a few days.

Distract yourself. You can reduce the intensity of your emotion by focusing your mind away from the situation or person upsetting you. Shift to another project, open your mail, watch television, go for a walk, catch up on filing, etc. Stare out the window. Read. Listen to the sound of traffic outside. Get your perceptions and your thoughts OFF the distressing topic momentarily, then return your focus when you are ready.

Do not let yourself become over-stimulated. If you are an emotional person, it helps to plan your day to avoid over-stimulation. Too many conversations, or too many negotiations, or too many complaints by employees can set you up. Some people choose not to listen to the morning news before work because it upsets them just before they need to be focused and calm.

Pick certain people with whom you can "vent." None of this is to say you are supposed to suppress all of your feelings. We all need to express our emotions. Some people are more expressive than others. To have a colleague (or friend outside the organization) with whom you can "vent" can be highly valuable. You can discharge the emotional energy to someone who will not react to it. This helps you calm down before facing the people who are more likely to react to your emotion.

Keep emotion out of emails. In ancient times (a few years ago), if you were upset by a letter you would have to type your response, fold the paper, put it in an envelope, address it, apply a stamp, and set it in the outgoing mailbox where it sat for a few hours. There was plenty of time to retrieve and edit it. Now you can type your impulsive, rage-filled response and hit "send" in seconds and *voila!*—the damage is done. Email allows almost no time to reflect. If you want to send an emotional email, store it for 24 hours, reread it, and then decide whether to send it. Better yet, use email for routine tasks (sending documents, confirming appointments) and pick up the phone or talk face-to-face if the topic is emotional. You're much more likely to work out the problem person-to-person.

Lead a balanced life. Living your life too much for your job can cause intense emotion at work. Bringing your personal problems to work can also lead to being seen as someone who is "too emotional." It is imperative to balance work and personal life, and to seek help from friends or professionals if a life crisis is causing you to overreact to situations at work.

Have a rehearsed phrase ready for slowing things down. Rehearse this phrase and have it ready for any situation in which you need to buy time to avoid over-reacting. "I'm going to take some time to carefully consider your perspective, and then I'd like to talk again soon." In highly tense situations, use this one: "This conversation is very upsetting. I'd like to take a break and resume it later."

LANGUAGE

♦ "I think we're both too emotional now to keep this conversation productive. Let's take a ten minute break."

♦ "I need to calm down. I don't want to say something I'll regret. I'll call you after I've thought about it."

♦ "I need time to process this news. I really don't want to share my reaction right now.

♦ "I'd rather not react until I know exactly what I'm reacting too. I need more information and time to consider it."

SELF-TALK

♦ *I don't like the way this meeting is going, but I'm not going to react right now.*

♦ *I'm starting to feel upset, but I'll keep breathing and staying calm and I'll think through the situation later.*

♦ *If I have to respond now, I'll say I need time to think.*

♦ *I need to think about this. Don't react now.*

♦ *How can I distract myself?*

♦ *With whom can I talk who will be detached?*

5. Fine Tune Your Truth Detector

Transparency:
Clarity about personal values,
a steady demonstration of integrity,
and a willingness to admit mistakes and
confront unethical behavior.

"If you tell the truth you don't have to
remember anything."
—Mark Twain

Stuart is the owner of a large medical practice. He also invests in other businesses, and is active on a non-profit board.

When you ask him to account for his financial and professional success, he talks about hard work, his marriage, and common sense. If you dig deeper, he'll tell you about his values of fairness, honesty, and his willingness to "complain."

"If I see something wrong or unfair, I can't live with myself unless I speak up." Though soft-spoken, Stuart can take an unpopular stand at meetings.

"I don't respect organizations or individuals who pledge themselves to noble values but behave as if their words are merely P.R. I couldn't respect myself if I made a mistake or a misjudgment and tried to hide it."

If you ask about the business outcomes of listening to his truth detector, he'll say he's been a pain in the neck to many people over the years. He'll say he's lost money at times. But he'll also tell you he succeeded partly due to the credibility and trust he built in his personal and professional relationships.

"I sleep very well."

Enhancing Transparency

There are hundreds if not thousands of career choices and leadership decisions you'll make in your lifetime. Many will be small and some will be large. You'll make many decisions about your career or your organization related to colleagues, projects, promotions, what to say or not to say at a meeting, whether or not to tell your boss about a mistake, as well as decisions about money. Career and leadership decisions are best guided by a well-formulated set of values and ethics. You'll also *observe* many people making many decisions. You'll see unethical behavior, sometimes minor and sometimes major. For both altruistic and self-serving reasons, your career and the lives of the people around you are best served by living transparently, and holding others to that standard.

ATTITUDES

- The long-term benefits of ethical leadership are more valuable than any short-term gain.

- Everybody makes mistakes. It's what you do about them that matters most.

- Having a clearly defined set of values, goals, and ethics is an intangible asset to yourself and your organization.

- Integrity is pragmatic.

- Transparency is not just an option; it's the way people of character conduct business.

- Honesty is the best policy.

ACTIONS

Stay in touch with your higher purpose. Write down what is more important to you in life. If money is on your list, dig deeper: why is money valuable to you? The purpose of a business and a career is not just to make money. Money is a necessity in our society but most people are driven by a higher purpose having to do with building something and/or supporting others. What is your purpose? How are you contributing to your organization beyond what technical skills you bring? What is your contribution to your community and society? How are you serving your family and friends? How are you making the world better? There is a nearly infinite number of ways to help the world. What is your way? Having a higher purpose in life—and a thought process that reminds you of how you contribute to the lives of others—makes it less likely that unethical opportunities will distract you.

Practice the Golden Rule. "Do unto others as you would have them do unto you." Imagine all business transactions guided by this simple, pragmatic maxim. Enron would still be in business.[9]

Review ethical dilemmas from your life. Look back on difficult decisions when the "right path" was not clear. What was your thought process? What did you do? Which of the following served as a source of guidance and strength when you faced a difficult ethical decision:

♦ Your religious beliefs?

♦ A philosophical perspective?

♦ Principles your parents taught you?

♦ A friend or partner's input?

♦ A particular role model?

♦ Empathy?

♦ Something or someone else?

Whatever served you well in maintaining your integrity and living with transparency was and is a valuable asset in your life. Return to it often.

Study a role model of transparency. Is there a historic figure who inspires you to live by your values? Is there someone in your life or in your past you can think of as a role model (teacher, family member, friend, leader, etc.)?

Think about where your integrity is soft. Think about an area of your life in which you are *not* transparent. Do you need to talk it out confidentially with someone in order to live in accordance with your stated values? What are the costs of compromising your transparency?

Confront unethical behavior. There are many ways of doing this. It depends on what the unethical behavior is, as well as the culture of your organization, as to how you should confront something. It may involve a simple conversation, or filing an anonymous complaint, or rallying other colleagues to help you challenge something.

Talk to a trusted friend about the mistakes you've made and what you learned from them. Living transparently does not mean you need to "confess" everything. Nor is it meant to promote perfectionism. But it often helps to re-examine things confidentially with someone you trust. Such discussions can give you the emotional room needed to examine and learn from misjudgments. Most people benefit from having a confidante, someone with whom they do not have to be careful about what they say or what they reveal about their thought process. It may be someone inside or outside your work. And it will likely take time to develop the trust necessary to be open about your flaws or mistakes. But if you take the time to develop such a relationship, it is likely to provide wisdom and practical advice.

Study the ethics of your field. If you are in a position of leadership, you have a greater responsibility than the average person to know the up-to-date thinking about your profession and/or your industry. Most professions and industries have an official set of ethics published by a related association. Stay up to date on yours.

Be a role model. When you live with integrity, you are affecting the culture of your organization. If a leader is seen as unethical, you can bet there are other members of the organization who see that as an endorsement for opportunism. Even if you are *very* ethical, but you never discuss the thought process behind some of your ethical decisions, the appearance might be one of secrecy or a neglect of such concerns.

Conduct your business as if "60 Minutes" was watching. Imagine you were going to be closely examined by the media, or an auditor, or Sherlock Holmes. Living transparently means you don't have to worry if people look closely at how you conduct your business.

LANGUAGE

- "Let's remind ourselves of our values."
- "I'm not comfortable with that."
- "What would our customers think of this?"
- "What example are we setting?"
- "What will be the long-term consequences?"
- "I need to let you know about a mistake I made."
- "One of my strongest values is to be up front with the client."

- "I feel very strongly that the right thing to do in a situation like this is to just be honest."
- "That's not something I can support."
- "I'd like to get input from all of you as to what the ethical thing to do is in this situation."

SELF-TALK

- *I've got to live with myself first.*
- *My personal integrity is more important than any specific job.*
- *I don't have to work somewhere that lacks integrity.*
- *What would my role model do in this situation?*
- *I don't have to go through this alone. I can talk to someone about this situation.*
- *I'm human. I goofed. What can I learn from this?*
- *That decision didn't turn out the way I thought it would. Here is an opportunity to learn and grow.*
- *It is not my job to be perfect. My job is to try to do my job well, and to recover and learn from setbacks.*

6. Always Play Your Part

Conscientiousness:
The ability to consistently handle
your responsibilities.

"It's not so much how busy you are,
but *why* you are busy.
The bee is praised; the mosquito is swatted."
—Marie O'Conner

Katherine is known in her company as someone you can count on to complete a project.

She rarely has to adjust a deadline, but when she does, everyone involved with the project is kept informed.

"I like to minimize guesswork and surprises."

Task-focused colleagues and managers are big fans. But not everyone is quick to cheer her on.

Some co-workers complained that she is *too* focused on the finish line. That she doesn't listen enough. Doesn't collaborate enough. Push, push, push.

"They're right," she says. "I can't say I like hearing that feedback, but neither can I dismiss it as nitpicking."

Katherine knows from 360's and other input that to advance in leadership she has to learn better rapport building.

"I know people aren't robots. I work with some types easily; others need more discussion and socializing."

While acknowledging her need to improve some of her people skills, she is uncompromising about her conscientious approach to her responsibilities.

"To me the #1 people skill is a do-your-job mentality. I believe it's important to always play your part so you get the job done and you don't let others down. People *trust* people who follow-through on things. If you can't handle your responsibilities, you weaken trust."

Enhancing Conscientiousness

Farmers don't get paid for the months of hard work leading up to the harvest. They get paid for the harvest itself, and they know it. Conscientious leaders also know that people don't really get paid just to work; they get paid to complete things. Conscientious people clearly see the connection between their specific contribution and the big outcome. Whether your job is simple and repetitive or complex and varied, your organization needs you to play your part in getting things done and to effectively manage several tasks. Conscientious people help an organization attract and retain customers and revenue. Conscientiousness is more than good intentions. It is a set of work habits, as well as mental and emotional discipline, that help you stay on track and work with other team members toward the completion of clear goals. Being known as conscientious is good for your reputation and good for your organization's reputation. It gives individuals more career options, and it gives organizations a competitive edge.

ATTITUDES

♦ Others are counting on me to do my part.

♦ Effectively managing my responsibilities is a major part of what makes me a professional.

- I am a leader. Others are watching me for the example I set on work ethic and getting things done.
- I take personal responsibility for my job and my professional standards.

ACTIONS

Employ the "First 15 Technique." Try this. Spend the first 15 minutes of your workday prioritizing. Consider all you *should* do that day, and then make decisions regarding what you *can* do. You'll know whether you need to do some rescheduling, delegating, or re-prioritizing. That "First 15" will cost you a little more than one hour per week, but will save you many hours per month and help you focus.[10]

Ask often: "What's the main thing?" There are too many things to do. But many tasks are busy work. What is the main thing your job is supposed to accomplish? Ask yourself that question often and use the answer to push some work off your desk. Trying to be conscientious about *everything* is inefficient, unfocused, and perfectionistic.

Break down tasks into their parts; set smaller goals. Every task is actually a collection of tasks. If your goal is to complete a section of a report by the end of the day, you'll be that much more motivated and organized as you face the next section the following day.

Utilize technology. There are many computer programs and cell phone gimmicks you can use to remind yourself of things you have to do. "I forgot" is not an excuse in the information age.

Delegate and forget. If you can't stop worrying about a delegated task, you haven't full delegated it. Effective delegation involves "accountability loops." For loose loops, have your delegates take actions they think are appropriate, and inform you *afterwards*. For tighter loops, have delegates inform you *beforehand* as to any action they plan to take. When the stakes are high, schedule a follow-up meeting for the delegate to give you a complete report on the delegated task. By taking these steps, you can delegate something and forget it. You'll get an update in time to address problems. "Trust but verify."

Trust the team. If you neglect certain kinds of tasks, talk to your team. The power of a team involves building on strengths and compensating for each other's weaknesses. Maybe you are conscientious about some tasks and not others. Tell your team when you are likely to run to the goal and when you are likely to "drop the ball." Work together to create a conscientious system that's effective *and* fair.

Model it. If you are in leadership and you look like you don't get your own work done, you are sending the wrong message. High expectations motivate people only if the leader lives up to them.

Practice assertiveness often.

♦ **Positive assertiveness:** This is the ability to say clearly and directly what you want. You are more likely to manage your responsibilities if you can assertively ask for help, feedback, realistic deadlines, additional resources, etc.

♦ **Negative assertiveness:** This is the ability to say "no." Conscientious people say "no" to the responsibilities that do not belong to them so they can focus on the responsibilities that do.[11]

Discuss connections between specific responsibilities and larger business outcomes. Many years ago everyone saw an uncomplicated connection between what they did and how it created results (e.g. the town blacksmith). But organizations are now larger and more complex than ever. Discussing how day-by-day work contributes to the organization's success helps everyone see the value and necessity of what they do. It helps them focus on higher value tasks. It can motivate people by making them feel more connected to a larger purpose. And it can help people advance their careers by learning to articulate their contribution.

Know what is *not* your responsibility. Some people mismanage their responsibilities by taking on others'. While it is well intentioned (and occasionally necessary) to go outside of your job to assist others, conscientious people have clear boundaries about what needs to get done and what is really up to someone else. Conscientious people would rather point someone to a fishing pole than hand out fish.

Hold others accountable. Value conscientiousness. Don't shift work from your least conscientious people to your most conscientious. In the short run you'll get more done, but you'll punish the best performers. Keep doing that and they'll find a better job.

Ask yourself, "Am I doing what I love to do?" Some people wonder why they can't seem to get their work done—and eventually realize they are chasing someone else's dream. Are you in leadership only because of the salary? Are you running a business you inherited but don't enjoy? Are you an engineer only because your father was one? It's difficult to be conscientious if you do not have a natural desire for the work. "Do what you love and the money will follow."[12]

LANGUAGE

♦ "I'd like to talk to you about how we can complete this project on time."

- "I want both of us to succeed; let's look at what needs to be done and who is most suited to do it."
- "I need your help on this."
- "I've been waiting for your report, and I need to know when I can expect to see it completed."
- "I know you have a lot to juggle. So let's sit down and plan how to get this finished."
- "I'd like to help you, but I'm focused on something else right now."
- "I'm up against a deadline. You'll need to ask for help from someone else."
- "No, I'm not willing to do that. I've got enough on my plate now."
- "As I said, I'm not willing to do that."
- "This is *your* responsibility."

SELF-TALK

- *What is the most valuable thing I can focus on today?*
- *What responsibilities will I be neglecting if I start something new right now?*
- *Is this request for my time directly related to my responsibilities?*
- *Do I need help with this and I'm not admitting it?*
- *I am a professional; I can manage this.*
- *Stay focused.*

7. Learn How To Bounce

Resilience:

Adjusting to change, surmounting obstacles,

practicing flexible thinking,

and tolerating ambiguities.

"Trouble is only opportunity in work clothes."

—Henry J. Kaiser

"We've been through a merger, two reorganizations, and countless new initiatives in less than five years. Every time I turn around someone moves my cheese."

Linda manages a team of scientists, engineers, and other managers. "Some of my people adapt well to change because they understand our industry. Others do well because that's the kind of people they are. Still others adapt because they learn certain skills. And a few just can't adapt. They probably won't be around long."

Linda is patient with those who have difficulty adapting—up to a point.

"I need people who can free themselves from all-or-nothing thinking patterns. When someone focuses on the company's contradictions, or repeatedly complains about uncertainties we're facing, I think: 'Do they expect me to control the whole company, or our market, or even the economy?' I need them to understand that most of the changes we face are created by forces beyond our control."

Her own ability to remain resilient and flexible in the face of frequent change is based on a strong belief: "What is always in our control is how we *respond* to change."

Enhancing Resilience

Change is not an option. Your organization, your community, your family, and our entire society are all changing and you can't stop it. What you *can* do is develop resilience. This is a competency for adapting to and guiding change. Having a positive attitude and the ability to think with flexibility keep you from feeling like a victim of change. Approaching obstacles ready to ask for help and thinking creatively helps reduce anxiety. Organizations with resilient people are more likely to adapt to a quickly changing market. Individuals with this competency are happier when they get home from work, and more likely to generate career options.[13]

ATTITUDES

♦ Change affects everybody; don't take it personally.

♦ It is important to be flexible and resilient during times of change.

♦ *Pro*active is more effective than *re*active.

♦ People need encouragement during change.

ACTIONS

Understand why people struggle with change:

♦ **Loss of control is at the heart of change.** We all need a sense of control in our lives. When large forces around us are changing, we feel less in control of our own lives. At worst, we feel helpless.

♦ **Adapting to change often means recovering from a significant disruption in expectations.** What you *expect* to happen has a lot to do with how you *feel* about what happens. When what you think will happen doesn't happen, you have to adjust mentally.

♦ **A lack of resilience will probably show up as dysfunctional behavior.** When change occurs and people cannot adjust their outlook or behavior, this can produce symptoms of depression, anxiety, aggression, denial, defensiveness, low productivity, physical illness, etc.

♦ **People tend to view change as either a danger or an opportunity.** Flexible optimism is the ideal state of mind for facing change. Mild pessimism makes things harder but can work. Rigid or extreme pessimism makes change much harder.

Understand the characteristics of resilience:

♦ **Positive view of yourself and the world.** This means you accept yourself for who you are and you are basically a trusting, optimistic person.

♦ **Remaining focused.** This is the ability to stick to priorities and not to get easily distracted.

♦ **Flexible in behavior and expectations.** The more fixed or rigid you are in your behavior patterns and expectations, the more out of control you will feel if situations surprise you. It is inevitable that you will have expectations, but the quicker you can adjust them with new information, the better. As you adjust your thoughts, you can adjust your behavior appropriately.

♦ **Getting and staying organized.** Change does not demand that we are perfectly organized, but it does demand that we are organized *enough*. As hard as change is, chaos makes it harder.

♦ **Proactive more than reactive.** You can't control everything, but you can try to *influence* things. Proactive behavior is more likely to be effective, and even when you don't get what you want you will feel better for having tried. Lack of proactive efforts can result in a sense of helplessness.

Know your quota for change. Imagine that you have 100 change points each year. Every change, big or small, positive or negative, requires that you use some of your points. Knowing how many "points" you spend is valuable self-awareness. While resilience is a good thing, it is also good to be realistic about your limitations and to take steps to keep from getting overwhelmed.

Review your style of dealing with change. Write down some of the major changes you've faced in the last few years. Identify your change-related patterns of thinking, emotion, and behavior. What aspects of your patterns work quite well? What aspects do you see clearly as limiting your ability to adapt effectively?

Allow yourself and others time to acclimate. Change may not be your choice, but you do have some choices regarding how quickly you must adapt. As a leader, knowing that the people around you adapt at various rates can help you be understanding of resistance. Some changes, of course, have to be sudden and give people little time to adapt. But most changes leave some time to implement strategies for reducing the stress.

Be ready for resistance. Whether you are in leadership or on a team—and even if the change is positive—accept the fact that people will resist change. This comes from our need for consistency and stability. In other words, resistance is normal. The issue is *how much* some people (or even you) resist, and *how*. When you observe resistance, discuss it openly and try to find out what the person needs to "get on board." Some people will appreciate such discussions and become more adaptive as they perceive their needs being taken seriously. Some small percentage of people will never stop resisting and may become very problematic.

Recognize your own negative emotions as early warning signs. When you feel anxious or angry, pay attention. You don't have to act on those emotions, at least not impulsively. Nor do you need to obsess on these emotions. But they are telling you that you need support, clarification or relaxation. You will be less effective in adapting to change (or helping others to do so) if you completely ignore or deny negative emotions.

Manage frustration when facing obstacles. When you get frustrated, review the benefits and opportunities that will come with determination and success. Don't fight change, figure out how to use it and benefit from it. If your frustration builds up to the point that you're frequently barking at people, you'll make your situation worse.

Think of yourself as self-employed with one client. Do not get addicted to one organization. Be ready to adapt to the evolving job market by keeping your résumé up to date and always working on marketable skills.

Market yourself internally. Continually observe your organization for what is perceived as valuable. Invent ways to add value and tactfully remind others of what you contribute. Take advantage, when possible, of changes internal to your organization.

Build resilient teams and organizations. This is done by recruiting resilient individuals and by combining people who compliment each other on the characteristics of resilience. When a group of people can leverage their strengths and compensate for their weaknesses, they can help each other (and the entire organization) adapt to and take advantage of change. Characteristics of resilient teams and organizations include resilient individuals, willingness to work with ambiguity, creative use of tension, self-organizing units (groups that do not just wait for orders), competence, and mutual support.

LANGUAGE

♦ "Who has an idea of how we can make this change work for us?"

♦ "Let's see how flexible we can be so we can accomplish our ultimate goal."

♦ "I know this situation has a lot of uncertainty, so let's clarify what we know and what we need to find out."

SELF-TALK

♦ *These obstacles are a challenge, and I will succeed.*

♦ *I need to learn a new skill to effectively deal with this challenge. I can do that.*

♦ *How can I create an opportunity from this change?*

8. Leverage Your Desire Portfolio

Achievement orientation:
The passionate commitment to satisfy one's
own benchmark of high quality,
and a hunger for learning.

"To love what you do and feel that it matters,
how could anything be more fun?"
—Katherine Graham

"People respond to my high expectations in one of two ways: they complain or they thank me."

Carla is driven by a passion for her work, high standards, and a zeal for learning. When hired by a non-profit to turn things around, she told them she wasn't a top down turnaround specialist.

"If I can improve this organization, it will take time. I use a command style of leadership only in a crisis or with non-collaborative employees. My method is to steadily raise the bar on how we view our mission and serve our constituents."

Long before she entered management, coworkers saw her as a change agent. They said things like: "When you work for Carla, you end up giving your best because you know she's giving hers. You feel stretched and frustrated for a while, but in time you see yourself as a more competent and proud professional."

One reason for her high standards is her hunger for learning.

"I'll never stop studying leadership. Some folks think I'm just trying to reach the top of the ladder. But in my mind, I'm trying to reach my top potential and help others do so. It's part of my purpose in life."

Enhancing Achievement Orientation

Achievement orientation in the context of emotional intelligence is not synonymous with ambition. It is not about being workaholic. It is distinct from power hungry narcissism. Nor is it an obsession with status or financial gain. People who manifest the competency of achievement orientation are more likely to achieve higher levels of career success and leadership, but that is typically *not* what drives them. They are driven by a *passion* for high quality, for contributing value, and for life-long learning. The benefit to individuals is career success and a sense of pride and fascination for what they do. The benefit to the organization is the energy of passion, as well as higher standards, higher expectations, better service, and better leadership.

ATTITUDES

- I work because I need to contribute.
- I have a purpose beyond simply making a living or getting promoted.
- I have an internal standard of quality to which I am committed.
- I love to learn. I'll never stop learning.
- My career is a series of opportunities to contribute, to learn, and to grow.

ACTIONS

Imagine someone introducing you at your retirement party. What do you hope the speaker will say about you? What did you achieve? What did you stand for? What level of your career did you reach? How is the organization—and even the world—better because of your career? Whose lives were improved by your work? Answer all of these questions as you would like to hear them years from now.

What are your standards? Take a few minutes to put pen to paper about your internal standards related to your work. Forget, temporarily, what standards are imposed upon you. Define specifically the things you need to do in order to excel at work according to your own sense of quality. After describing your standards in writing, candidly assess to what extent, on a scale of 1 to 10, you strive each day to live up to your own standards. Now focus on your emotional reaction to your self-assessment. Imagine increasing your tendency to reach for your own standards daily, and how you might increase your sense of passion and pride.

Identify what you want to build. Of course you need to build your 401K and your résumé. But what else do you strive to build? What stimulates your passion? A company? Innovation? Your family? A charity? Healthy, smart children? Great friendships? Why do you go to work? Jot down some deeper reasons for doing what you do. What do you want to look back on ten years from now and feel proud of? What will be your legacy? Put them on a calendar or in your PDA for an annual review, if not more often. This is motivational rocket fuel.

Set specific, feasible goals. Where do you need to direct your passion in the short term, the next few months or year. What are the next few steps you need to take to move forward toward larger goals? Write down your top three goals for the short-term. Be specific and talk them over with your manager, a colleague, or friend. Make them feasible. If they are too lofty, it will be too easy to excuse yourself for not achieving them (e.g. "No wonder I didn't reach that goal, it was too much of a stretch").

Set learning goals. In addition to tasks you intend to complete, where are you setting your sights regarding new skills, new insights? How can you sharpen your professional abilities? Make a list of skills and knowledge you want to learn in the next year. Set it up in such a way that you hold yourself responsible for new learning.

Set deeper growth goals. How are you developing as a person? In addition to technical skills and intellectual learning, are you working toward becoming wiser? Are you gaining understanding about people and emotions? This kind of learning is just as applicable to your work and your life satisfaction as traditional learning. Talk with a close colleague or friend about how you intend to grow. Or ask for ideas.

Identify where you may be stagnant. You don't have to learn everything. Perfectionism is counterproductive. But what are you neglecting that is getting in the way of having a great life and a satisfying career? What are you denying or avoiding? Get some feedback from colleagues and loved ones.

Clarify for yourself what you contribute. Aside from your official job description, have you thought about what you truly contribute to your organization, team, or community? Make a list of your tangible and intangible contributions. Tangible contributions include your technical skills and professional expertise. Intangible contributions include the spirit you bring to a team, your humor, your integrity, people skills, curiosity, etc. Devise a way to make sure you review and revise this list annually.

Is it possible to improve your contributions and still have a balanced and pleasurable life? How else could you contribute, tangibly or intangibly, that wouldn't demand too much of your personal life? Is there more of your personality or values you could share with co-workers? Could you be more involved with a team? Are you taking as much leadership as you are capable of? Are you mentoring others?

Obsess on "added value." Resist the autopilot mentality of showing up for work and doing what you are told to do. Reject the concept of "coasting." Within each job description is latitude for choice and focus. Think like a business owner even if you are an employee of a giant organization. Your business is your career—and your success is based on identifying the most valuable contributions you can make in the marketplace where you work.

Try to identify your "mental glitches." All of us have beliefs and assumptions that hold us back from greater achievement. These mental glitches can be about people, gender, money, authority, opportunity—nearly anything. And the problem is they lurk in our subconscious, out of our awareness but nonetheless affecting our confidence and drive. Only through gut honest discussions with great listeners can we become aware of how we hold ourselves back—and begin to change.

LANGUAGE

♦ "I want to be involved with this project because I think I have something important to contribute."

♦ "As a team, we can do better. I think we need to stretch ourselves."

♦ "As my manager (or mentor or coach), I'd like you to help me set some goals for myself."

♦ "I'd like to assist you on that project because there are some important skills I will be able to learn."

♦ "I know I push. I know I have high expectations of the people who work for me. And if I'm unfair or ineffective I want to hear about it. But I also know that you have grown in your skills this year partly *because* I pushed you."

SELF-TALK

♦ *What can I contribute in this situation?*

♦ *Am I meeting my own standards here?*

♦ *I can do better if I clearly identify what the optimum outcome should be.*

♦ *What can I learn from this project?*

♦ *What can I get more involved in that will stimulate me and/or set me up for future career opportunities?*

9. Jumpstart Yourself & Others

Initiative:

A readiness to generate
and act upon new opportunities.

"I never notice what has been done.
I only see what remains to be done."

—Madam Curie

Sam sold his manufacturing firm and retired at forty-nine, set for life. For a year he traveled, socialized, and celebrated.

Life was good.

Life was _so_ good he had only one problem: boredom.

One day, when he was restless and world-weary, someone asked what he would do if he woke up penniless.

The question energized him.

"I'd start over," he said with a smile. "I'd have fun looking for opportunities."

"You don't have to go broke to do that," the someone said.

A year of stored up _oomph_ was suddenly released.

Sam can walk into any business and in minutes spark opportunities for expanding or innovating. He can see a gap in the market, or what's missing in a team. He knows what people want before they do. He developed his enterprising talents through mentors and mistakes he made during twenty years as a business leader.

His new ventures make money, though that's not why he's working again. (Please don't mention that to his investment partners). While his initiative brings him additional success, he's in it for the vitality.

Enhancing Initiative

Entrepreneurs create and seize opportunities in the marketplace. "Intrapreneurs" create and seize opportunities *within* an organization. Everyone, however, from the executive to the factory worker, has opportunities they can notice or ignore. This emotional intelligence competency is about seeing what is around you and what is missing. It is about sensing and feeling what people need and will respond to. It's about reading people and situations so well that you know just what's needed to "jumpstart" people and get them focused. While every organization needs many people who loyally and steadily carry out plans and procedures, they also need people who can create sparks. Individuals who develop this competency spend very little time bored. They make things happen and enjoy the excitement that comes with innovation. Organizations benefit from increased creativity and energy, and better ideas for surviving and thriving in tough times.

ATTITUDES

- Carpe diem!
- My work is a place to discover and create things.
- I don't have to wait for others; I can make things happen.

- It is better to apologize afterwards than to ask permission beforehand.
- Work is an adventure.
- Work is play.
- There has got to be a way of looking at this that will generate an opportunity.
- There is always a better way to do something.
- Life is an endless series of opportunities.
- This is a great opportunity; let's go!

ACTIONS

Don't crush what you want to grow. You may be a leader with so much initiative that you discourage initiative in others. If you practice a command style of leadership, be careful. You can unintentionally create dependence and passivity. Command style leadership works great in crisis situations and turnarounds. But if you want to develop and reward initiative in others, you have to mix command style with coaching and democratic styles of leadership.

Ask people what they want that they don't have. People with initiative are often skilled at asking questions that draw out information pointing to new opportunities. Practice conversing with people in a way that helps you discover their dreams, desires, and goals. Don't jump to solutions. Just listen and ask questions driven by curiosity.

Later, think about the conversation from a creative problem-solving perspective. Be patient. It might take ten of these conversations before you discover a useful idea. Practice this interviewing and thinking method over and over.

Fish with the right bait. To awaken initiative in others, it's important to spend time trying to figure out what will unlock each individual's creativity and motivation. Everybody wants something. Everybody. But it's not always obvious what motivates a specific person. One person is driven by a need for security. The next person is looking for stimulation. A third person might be looking for approval. Still another wants financial gain or status. If you can find the right bait, you can catch the people who work for you. You can unlock each person's motivational and thus bring out the best in them and your organization.

- If several people talk about their kids, you might be able to think of an initiative about work and family that gets people moving.

- Another person speaks frequently about financial goals; think about how to offer that person such incentives.

- Yet another person gets energized in discussions about travel. How can you create an opportunity for this person that electrifies him or her?

Listen in a different way for people's complaints and frustrations. When someone is "venting," you might hear an opportunity. In management you might hear the germ of an idea for reorganizing a department or team. In small business you might hear a way to improve customer service. In the professions, you might hear a way to distinguish yourself from the other lawyers or accountants in town.

Listen to people's fantasies. People tend to giggle and announce their wishful thinking aloud. At some point in history an entrepreneur overheard someone fantasizing about "paid vacations." That entrepreneur then figured out he could divide a person's salary by 52 instead of 50 and offer a two-week "paid" vacation. For a while that person probably cornered the labor market. This is not to suggest you trick your employees or colleagues. It is to encourage you to derive workable ideas from the things people would rub a genie's lamp for if they could.

Understand that different personalities offer different opportunities. Your initiatives will only work in the context of personality. A great idea that will motivate outgoing sales people will fall flat with introverted scientists, and vice versa.

"Begin with the end in mind."[14] Stephen Covey said it best. Focus first on the ultimate prize; then figure out the steps. Steps don't inspire initiative—some will be down-right boring. Steps are often a mundane means to an end. By starting with (and returning to) a mental picture of what you value and want to accomplish, you will energize yourself and others over and over again.

Think new thoughts. If initiative is not one of your strengths and you want to develop it, do nearly anything that will get you to think off track. Talk to people you usually don't talk to. Drive a different route to work. Read a book that shakes you up. Seek someone to talk to who encourages you to think aloud without much editing. Attend a workshop that challenges your thinking. Work with a coach who challenges your assumptions and your comfort. Find someone who really appreciates creative thought and let them shake up your thinking.

LANGUAGE

◆ "Let's look at this in a new way."

◆ "Let's brainstorm. Forget for a while what's realistic or practical; let's play with some ideas—no matter how absurd—that might free up our minds and lead us to a new solution or opportunity."

◆ "I know we've always done it that way. But our results have been mediocre. Let's find a better way."

◆ "We can do better. Let's figure it out."

- "I see an opportunity and I want you to listen to me with an open mind."
- "I like the way you think. I disagree with some of your ideas and conclusions, but I like it that you challenge me and the team. I want you to keep asking those creative questions at our meetings."

SELF-TALK

- *Just because people are upset does not mean this is a bad idea.*
- *I may be shaking things up, but it is for the ultimate purpose of innovating and improving.*
- *Think upside down and sideways. Think creatively about new ways to get things done.*
- *There is probably an opportunity here, whether I can see it or not.*
- *The way we've been doing things around here can definitely be improved.*
- *I'm ready to grab something if it looks like a great opportunity.*
- *I'm bored. Why am I settling for this?*

Part Three:
People Radar

10. Drink From The Glass That's Half Full

Optimism:

The tendency to have a positive outlook
about life and the future.

"I would rather stay positive and get 60% good results
than stay negative and get 100% bad results."

—Joyce Meyer

"I'm an optimist with my feet on the ground," says James. "Sure, I believe life usually works out great. I believe people are basically good. But it's also true that most businesses fail, and most products don't earn profit."

James is irritated by what he calls "autopilot optimists."

"When I hear the phrase 'this can't fail,' I know we're in trouble.

"Failure can be a form of feedback, but only if you first acknowledge a failure, and then candidly examine your contributions to what went wrong."

He claims that some of his colleagues—and even some of his company's officers—rationalize or deny obvious failure. He says they attribute it to bad luck, or say things like "we just have to move on," or "the market wasn't ready for us."

"In business you have to learn *flexible* optimism," he insists. "You have to make some mistakes, and discover how to run pilot projects that reveal your oversights and naiveté. Then, with good information and a strong team that includes a few skeptics, you can come up with a plan that's worthy of an optimist's enthusiasm."

Enhancing Optimism

Optimism is both a disposition and something you can learn. Some people learn it more easily than others. Optimism increases the probability of opening your eyes to opportunities. It helps you see the potential in others. It energizes you to face problems and challenges. It is motivational. Optimism also protects you psychologically from the negative emotions that come with failure, because you are more likely to see a failure as merely a temporary setback on the path to success. It strengthens leadership because people would rather follow an optimist than a pessimist.

ATTITUDES

♦ In the big picture, things work out.

♦ A strong team can solve problems.

♦ Setbacks are temporary.

ACTIONS

To increase optimism, choose an optimistic mentor with whom you can discuss decisions and predications. Choose someone who won't merely debate you to make you wrong, but rather weighs information *with* you. Listen to how this person's mind works so as to arrive at optimistic predictions and interpretations. Get the optimist to articulate why he or she is optimistic. Try applying this mental process to a low stakes situation and "experiment" with a more optimistic approach.

Beware of the dark side of optimism. Optimism can be a disguised form of denial or avoidance. Maintaining optimism in the face of ambiguous information is one thing, but some "optimistic" individuals can be foolhardy when they ignore obvious red flags. Some leaders get too emboldened by success and their optimism evolves into narcissism—they come to believe they are never wrong. Companies, military campaigns, and investments can be derailed by rigid optimism. Leaders can heed pessimism when it is warranted, without becoming chronic pessimists.

If you are sometimes blinded by too much optimism, you might want to temper it. If so, choose a mentor who is not chronically pessimistic, but is careful and analytical in his or her approach to decisions and challenges. If the person is merely a naysayer, you will take opposite positions and argue. Select someone with an open mind who has a talent for critical thinking. Make sure it's someone who can find the flaws or the danger in a situation, but isn't overly invested in shooting down creative or risky ideas. You don't have to agree with such a person, but he or she is likely to round out your approach to decision-making and help identify challenges that lie ahead. Many effective optimists seek alternative and critical perspectives.

Develop flexible optimism.[15] *Flexible* optimists maintain an overall positive view of the big picture, but acknowledge that there are times for caution and even retreat. While they have a bias for positive interpretations of events, they nonetheless seek multiple viewpoints and enough factual information that they can test their beliefs. To develop flexible optimism in yourself or someone else, ask these four questions about a prediction or upcoming decision.

1. **What is the *evidence* for my prediction?** This stimulates rational analysis of information.

2. **What *alternatives* make sense, given this evidence?** This stimulates an open mind and balanced consideration.

3. **What are the *implications* of my decision or prediction?** This simulates an examination of consequences and a clearer view of what is at stake.

4. **What is more *useful* now, optimism or pessimism?** In most cases, optimism is more useful, but not always.

Distinguish between decision-oriented optimism and philosophical optimism—then cultivate both. In personal and professional life, it helps to apply an optimistic perspective to decisions and predictions. An even bigger form of optimism is the big belief that life is good, that people are well-intentioned, and that life is meaningful and worth living. No matter what happens in your business or professional life, cultivating philosophical optimism through meaningful relationships, spirituality, and a love for life is a powerfully aspect of happiness and effectiveness.

Keep a record of your predictions. Whether it's investing in the stock market, or something related to your work, keep track of what you predict will happen in several situations. Look back at your recorded predictions later to see if you have a subconscious bias in favor of or contrary to optimism. Don't trust your unrecorded memory.

Study your own history. Look at your personal history, possibly with the help of a trusted confidante, to candidly assess the role of optimism or pessimism in your life. Do you predict negative outcomes too often in order to avoid disappointment? If so, what does this approach cost you in terms of opportunities and excitement? Is there another way to deal with life's inevitable disappointments other than defensive pessimism? Or, do you have a flexible optimistic attitude that keeps you open and motivated, and that you can temper when the situation calls for caution? If so, how do you regulate your optimism? Or, do you get feedback that you are unrealistic, too optimistic, or even "reckless." If you hear a pattern of this feedback, try to gain insight into your motives for exclusively predicting positive outcomes. Some people feel intensely uncomfortable with negative emotion and/or conflict. They jump to optimism too often and too quickly. It feels good in the short run but costs resources and strife in the long run.

Cultivate an organizational culture of optimism. If you are in leadership at any level, you can help others and yourself by voicing your optimism. Challenge others who *consistently* promote pessimism. Articulate thoughtful reasons for your positive predictions. Frequently communicate with your associates why you think a certain course of action will work out, and why it is worth the risks. You can also influence an organizational culture toward optimism by focusing on these three crucial tasks.

1. **Selection:** When you hire or promote, seek optimistic individuals.

2. **Placement:** When you make assignments, consider where optimists and mild pessimists have greater value. Sales people face frequent rejection and keep trying only if they can maintain optimism. Cost estimating is probably best served by conservative or mildly pessimistic predictions.

3. **Developing optimism:** Through coaching and other
    means of development, leaders can be guided to learn
    optimism.

LANGUAGE

♦ "I'm not sure how we'll get from point "A" to point
"B", but I think we'll figure it out."

♦ "I believe in our mission and I believe in our abilities.
Let's see how we can make this happen."

♦ "Here are my reasons for optimism . . ."

♦ "How did we come to this conclusion?"

♦ "What has been our record on this?"

SELF-TALK

♦ *I've been in these tough situations before. This is a set-back, but it is not the ultimate outcome.*

♦ *The fact that I am a bit nervous about this does not mean that it won't work. I've thought this through carefully and have enough information to proceed with optimism even though it's a stressful situation.*

♦ *This idea might just work—and if it doesn't, I'll learn something important.*

♦ *Why am I the most optimistic voice in this room right now? Are they not listening to me, or am I not really considering what they are saying?*

♦ *Life is good.*

11. Extend Your Personal Antenna

Empathy:

Understanding others' emotions, needs, and viewpoints, and acting upon others' concerns.

"Seek first to understand, and then to be understood."

—Steven Covey

Joanne manages a team of fundraisers for a non-profit. She also frequently asks people for large sums of money. One approach that definitely does not work when asking for a donation is the stereotypical persuasive sales pitch.

"I guess I'm in sales, but I don't feel like I 'sell' anything. If I listen to potential donors with empathy, they're more likely to come to a gift decision they feel good about and may repeat later. If I'm really tracking the subtleties of emotion, and truly listening to the fine points of meaning, I get valuable information on how to stay in touch, how to alter our approach, and what concerns to address in the future.

"I'm also a manager. I talk to my people all over the country. Most of them have families, aging parents, career goals, and an emotional commitment to our organization. When I stay in tune with these aspects of the people I lead, we are a stronger and more productive team. When we're out of harmony, our numbers are not as good."

Joanne enhanced her empathy skills as a minister. "I practice a different ministry now. I never thought I'd say this, but the empathy I learned through the ministry helped prepare me to become a better businesswoman and leader."

Enhancing Empathy

Empathy is an advantage in business and in your personal life. It's the basis for good customer service, win-win negotiation, friendship, and for helping employees grow and develop. Empathy also increases the probability of collaborative discussion and constructive action within partnerships and teams. Leaders who express empathy evoke inspired cooperation and make productivity much more likely. Empathy adds to a positive workplace climate. The bottom line: empathy is pragmatic.

ATTITUDES

♦ People matter. And their emotions matter.

♦ There is always more than one reasonable perspective on anything.

♦ It is pragmatic to deal with people's emotions.

ACTIONS

Understand the three types of empathy:[16]

1. **Cognitive empathy** occurs when you *recognize* another person's point of view—*and* his emotional reaction to it. This is the empathy that therapists, coaches, and skilled leaders often demonstrate through reflective listening. They paraphrase or summarize what a person just said, then focus on the person's emotional reactions. It is a concentrated way to build rapport and trust rapidly. If it is overused, however,

it can sound artificial. Most empathy is more naturally expressed through facial expressions, engaged listening, and comments that show you are taking the other person seriously. Cognitive empathy is the most basic and important type of empathy because it is through understanding others' perspectives and emotions that we develop many other people skills. NOTE: It is important to know that you do not have to get it "just right" when you are demonstrating cognitive empathy. If the other person perceives you as *trying* to understand (and not merely jumping to conclusions or judgments), he or she will let you know if you are misinterpreting something. Cognitive empathy is often a back-and-forth process that eventually results in mutual understanding.

2. **Emotional empathy** refers to actually feeling what another person is feeling. You demonstrate emotional empathy when, for example, someone tells you a sad story and you become tearful along with the storyteller, or you smile because someone looks so happy. While this can be an extremely powerful form of empathy, it is not as necessary as cognitive empathy.

3. **Compassionate empathy** is the most action-oriented of the three types. In compassionate empathy you take action to help others deal with an event and/or their reaction to it.

Example: You see that a colleague is frustrated with a task so you jump in to help and say something encouraging or soothing.

Assume positive intentions, unless there is evidence to the contrary. Most people are not trying to manipulate or exploit others. When there is conflict, you might incorrectly assume that the other person has negative intentions. This could prevent effective communication. Assume positive motives at first. This makes empathy easier.

Attempt to make all parties look positive. Everybody, including you, prefers to finish a conversation feeling good about themselves. Empathy is based partly on accurate meanings, but also on helping all parties "save face." You are more likely to get information that helps you empathize if you do and say things that help others preserve a positive self-image. People can disagree or make mistakes without being made to look incompetent or feel bad about themselves.

Hit the pause button on your emotions. If you are aware of frustration, anger, defensiveness, etc., resist too quick an emotional or verbal reaction. Otherwise, you might react to a meaning that the other person did not intend. If you have trouble putting your reactions on hold, practice this self-talk: "I need to hold my reactions until I really understand his/her perspective." Also refer to Competency #4: Emotional Self-Regulation. If you are perceived as not in control of your emotions, people will not even give you a chance to understand their perspective.

All parties must see the benefits of the next action. Even if a situation is not completely "win-win," all parties need some incentive to implement a decision. When working on a team, try to find solutions and goals that empathize with the needs and perspectives of all members. This increases motivation and builds stronger team relationships. Most people don't have to get their way, but they have to feel like their way is understood and being considered.

Practice "reflective listening." As mentioned above, this can help establish rapport quickly if not overused. Reflective listening involves paraphrasing (i.e. reflecting) a small part of what the other person says and then showing you understand their emotion. EXAMPLE: Person #1: "I can't believe I have to work this Saturday!" Person #2: "You have to work this Saturday? No wonder you're upset."

Choose actions that demonstrate interest in others' concerns. Empathy is not just about words and emotions and paraphrasing—it is also about actions. Examples: You do someone a favor when you know he's having a stressful day. Then you ask a follow-up question: "How is the project going? I know you were nervous about the deadline." While such a demonstration of empathy does not necessarily relate directly to getting the job done, it helps to forge bonds that pay off in morale and productive collaboration.

Negotiate for accurate understanding. People want to be understood. This is true of employees, customers, managers, board members, etc. People feel valued when they believe you are putting effort into getting a clear picture of what they mean, rather than a general impression of their perspective. Negotiating for accurate understanding is a back-and-forth discussion about what each person is trying to say. Here's the sequence:

1) Listen carefully with an open mind at first. Use thought empathy and/or emotion empathy as described above.

2) Verify and clarify. What exactly does the other person mean? "Do you mean _____, or do you mean _____?"

3) Repeat the process until the other person clearly indicates you are accurate in your understanding and interpretations.[17]

LANGUAGE

♦ "I'm not sure I understand your perspective; let's talk some more before we make a decision."

- "Help me understand what you mean by that. I'm still not clear."
- "I know what you mean. I've felt that way, too."
- "Yes, I can see that. What you're saying makes sense."
- "I don't agree with you, but I can definitely understand your perspective."
- "You and I disagree on a several aspects of this discussion, but let me tell you what is reasonable about what you're saying."
- "I really want to understand your point of view. I think it's important that we keep trying. Please explain to me again how you see this."

SELF-TALK

- *What would it feel like to be in the other person's situation right now?*
- *What would I be thinking and feeling if our roles were reversed?*
- *What is reasonable about the other person's perspective, even if I don't see it the same way?*
- *If we keep working to understand each other, we're more likely to find a solution that works for both of us.*

12. Become A Major Contributor

Service Orientation

A commitment to serve customers, and to support others who serve customers.

"From the start, our entire business—from design to manufacturing to sales—was oriented around listening to the customer."

—Michael Dell

"I'm passionate about customer service. I'm devoted to supporting our customers *and* those who support them," asserts Nancy.

"I want everyone who works with us to treat customers as if the success of the corporation depends on them. Because in fact it does."

One of her colleagues once tried to convince Nancy she was taking some "minor" customer service problems too seriously.

"Some customers call our 800 number needing a baby-sitter," the colleague argued in frustration. "Sometimes they haven't even read the product's simple instructions."

"And how do you distinguish a 'baby' from a mature repeat customer who has too many things on her mind that day?" responded Nancy.

"I consider us partners with our customers," she often says. "I want a mutually beneficial relationship with as many of them as possible for as long as possible."

She doesn't stop there.

"All of us—and our sales people especially—are in the business of making our customers' lives better. We need to really feel the need and the duty to passionately serve them. They are people coming to us asking for help."

Enhancing Service Orientation

The primary purpose of any organization—profit or non-profit—is to attract, maintain, and serve a clientele. Making money is necessary, but not a main purpose. Customers are attracted to people and organizations that meet their needs. Individuals, teams, and leaders with this emotional intelligence competency are "in tune" with customers. They connect with customers. And they get valuable information from customers. Furthermore, in today's service economy most products and services are commodities. Your competition can probably do what you do—for the same price if not lower. Your customers want more than a good product or service at a good price; they want to feel good about doing business with you. All organizations are in the business of selling positive emotional experiences. The ability to evoke positive emotions in customers translates into return business and organizational effectiveness.

ATTITUDES

- Customers and their needs are why we exist and grow.
- Think like a customer.
- Attract rather than persuade customers.
- Without a growing number of satisfied customers, this organization will decline or die.
- Our mission is service; our reward is revenue.

ACTIONS

Know *whom* you serve. This sounds obvious, but to many people it's not. Many people in organizations have only a vague idea of who the customer is, and/or little motivation to meet any more than a customer's minimum expectations. If you stop and think about who your customer is, you might realize you have several different levels of customers. For example, in health care there are patients, insurance companies, and corporate contracts. Schools have students, parents, and research grants. Serving every level of customers is part of attracting and retaining business.

Remind associates of whom they serve. The more clearly you know who your customers are, the more consistently you can remind others in your organization. When someone says they have to do something because the boss told them to, remind them that customer service is an even more basic motive.

Don't *guess* what customers want, *ask* them. Through surveys, focus groups, and other means, find out *exactly* what your customers want (and don't want). Find out what makes them feel good, and what irritates them. Service orientation requires good listening and empathy, but it also requires methodical inquiry.

Measure your feedback in some way. Collecting feedback is good; measuring and tracking customer satisfaction over time is better. Annual surveys help you determine if things are improving or not.

Conduct focus groups. A powerful way to learn about your customers *and* give them a positive emotional experience is to conduct focus groups. Step 1: Recruit a small number of customers (about 8 to 20) and put them in a room together. Step 2: Make them very comfortable. Serve good food. Step 3: Ask open questions about their experiences with your organization. Listen—and never get defensive or explain. Just listen and ask clarifying questions. Make them feel good for being honest with you, even if they say negative things or make petty complaints. Step 4: Implement one or more of their suggestions ASAP (something obvious such as new lighting). Complete other improvements as time and budget allows. This process will accomplish two things: you will get valuable information about your products or services, and you will be marketing to that small group. They will feel great that you listened to them and took some action they suggested.

Involve customers early in the process. Whether your organization creates products or services, find out early what the customer thinks and feels. Using the methods above (as well as others), seek your customers' reactions to upcoming changes or new offerings. Do it early. You'll save time, money, headaches, and failures.

Develop your "backstage" employees. Every organization has people who do important tasks but rarely face the customer. These people also work in customer service, but may not realize it. As a leader, look for opportunities for key "backstage" people to interact directly with clientele. You can bring customers in. You can have backstage employees accompany salespeople on calls, or sit in on focus groups. Get creative, and get them connected.

Shuffle the deck. Rotate people through jobs or duties in a way that everybody gets a turn working closer to the customer. Give people temporary assignments that will give them a new perspective on whom they ultimately serve. Letting people get overly focused in the same job (or rut) may be comfortable, but may deprive them of opportunities to develop service orientation.

Listen for the need behind the complaint. When a customer complains, there is the surface information (they had to wait too long, or the gizmo didn't work, etc.). But there is a deeper message about a personal need that's only being half-expressed. Maybe the customer needs an apology, or some encouragement. If you can hear the emotional need behind the complaint, you are much more likely to resolve the complaint. Resolving the complaint essentially means getting the customer to feel positive emotions again about doing business with your organization.

Develop real relationships with customers and ask for feedback. If you owned a grocery store and asked for feedback from a customer you didn't know well, you wouldn't learn much about your business. But if you talked to someone who had been shopping there for years and with whom you have a warm, conversational relationship, you would likely get some *very* useful information. Investing in real relationships pays off with pragmatic feedback.

Understand the emotional power of customers. From time to time, satisfied customers will mention your business to others. *Un*satisfied customers, on the other hand, will badmouth you frequently and passionately.

Reward and promote. Service orientation needs to be part of your organizational culture. If you reward and promote individuals who manifest this competency, you'll see more of it.

Don't forget your *potential* customers. If you want to grow, your current customers are not enough. Learn all you can about your competition's customers. What are their likes, dislikes, and values that you could use to turn them into *your* customers? Don't ignore them just because they don't buy from you. Study them. Interact with them. Listen.

Stay connected to your original inspiration. Nothing is as important to service orientation as a clear and consistent commitment to your original inspiration. Write a paragraph about why you chose your particular profession or industry. Whether you serve children, doctors, small business owners, etc., say why you care about this group of customers. What inspired you to start your business, or join this company or non-profit? After you write it, talk about it.

LANGUAGE

♦ "I would value your input on how we do business."

♦ "I promise you I won't take it personally if you give me some honest feedback on how I can do better."

♦ "I don't like it when one of my customers is not satisfied. How can I improve things for you?"

♦ "What do you need?"

SELF-TALK

♦ *How can I make this opportunity attractive and satisfying for this customer?*

♦ *Seek first to understand. If I don't understand my customers, it won't matter if they understand me.*

♦ *What is the need behind this customer's complaint?*

13. Listen To The Big Whisper

Organizational awareness:
The ability to discern the culture and climate of an organization, build effective personal networks, and navigate politics.

"Every company has two organizational structures:
The formal one is written on the charts;
the other is the everyday relationship of the
men and women in the organization."
—Harold S. Geneen

Harriet's strength had become a weakness.

She had a candid style. In all levels of meetings she politely but persuasively challenged others.

"She's sharp," commented her manager, Anne. "Very good at debate. Her comments are well conceived and definitely add to the discussion."

The company ostensibly values Harriet's style.

"But in practice," says Anne, "many of the other managers found it intimidating."

Anne likes Harriet's straightforward manner, "but in this context it was reducing her influence as a leader. People were tuning her out."

So Anne did some challenging of her own.

"I believed in Harriet, but was frustrated when she insisted she was merely practicing what the company preached," remembers Anne. "So I told her she would derail her career. She reminded me again of the organization's stated values. I confronted her to distinguish the ideal culture from the *real* one.

"She spoke privately to some key people after that, and figured out the actual culture and politics of our company. She still challenges others, but selectively. She's gaining credibility and is clearly more effective."

Enhancing Organizational Awareness

Today's organizations are complex. Each has its own culture, with stated and unstated values and rules. Each has official and unofficial political structures affecting which individuals and groups hold more power. Each has social networks that have nothing to do with the official org chart, but have everything to do with getting the right things done. Each has an "emotional economy"—the pattern of morale and motivation that drives or impedes effort. Complicating all of this is a state of ongoing change (e.g. markets, laws, leadership, etc.). Progress, as well as individual career success, requires sensitivity and savvy regarding all of this. Organizational awareness helps you make better predictions about resistance to and cooperation with your initiatives, and the likely outcomes of your efforts. An awareness of politics and social networks need *not* be associated with "cut throat" Machiavellian behavior. You can build social networks and navigate politics with integrity.

ATTITUDES

♦ Every organization has a style and culture.

♦ The invisible organization is important.

♦ You build an organizational culture or you get one.

♦ The emotional economy affects the bottom line.

♦ Staying connected in a network is vital.

- The *un*official culture affects everything.

- Navigating politics is often necessary.

- Power can be used without being abused.

ACTIONS

Study your organizational culture.[18] Culture is to an organization as personality is to an individual. Culture is made up of patterns. Patterns of values, beliefs, customs, myths and attitudes held by members. Culture influences the behavior of all individuals and groups. It has a strong impact on decision-making, distribution of resources, rewards, promotions, ethics, how people are treated, and ideas. Nonetheless, most organizations pay no attention to consciously shaping culture, or even describing it.

Describe **your organizational culture.** Brainstorm a list of words, values, or actions that describe your organization. This is best done in a group, if feasible. Next, write or discuss answers to the following questions. You will have a better understanding of your organization's culture.

- Who sets the style and pace of work? Who are the role models? Is it "do as we do" or "do as we say"?

- What behavior is rewarded, punished, or ignored? Is feedback frequent, intermittent, or never? Are unethical practices condoned through silence?

- What information is shared: that which is needed or merely that which leaders want to hear? Does information flow upward? Do leaders really know what is happening at all levels?

- How is high performance encouraged? What performance appraisal system is used? How is strong talent recruited? How strong is the commitment to training and development?

- Are stated values backed up by time and money?

- What is the relative importance of: Bottom line results? Saving face? Ego and power building? Positive workplace environment?

- How is constructive conflict managed? Is it overt? Is it resolved? Is it mediated? Is it buried? Is it punished?

- How are creative ideas received and rewarded?

- How important is workplace diversity and fairness?

- What is the balance between competition and collaboration?

Design **your organizational culture.** If you are in a position to actually influence your organizational culture, follow these steps.

Step 1: Ask yourself (and preferably a team of leaders) these three questions:

a) What does our market require?

b) What would we like to be?

c) How do these compare?

Step 2: Describe the patterns of attitudes and behaviors you want your organization to reward (internally and externally).

Step 3: Describe which rewards generally matter most to people in your organization (e.g. money, promotion, opportunities, training, stimulating assignments, benefits, team membership, etc.)

Step 4: Create a plan for implementing your ideas.

Step 5: Activate the plan.

Understand the nature of politics. As often as we hear the word "politics" in the media, it is easy to forget what it essentially is. Politics is about power and authority. Someone with political power can get others to do things. Someone can get political power by holding a title, by controlling money, by influencing careers, by collaborating with others who hold power, etc. Someone can also influence emotions and thus gain political power by evoking fear, inspiration, prejudice, greed, enthusiasm, etc.

Navigate politics. Thinking and acting politically can be done with character and integrity. A great idea can get killed if it is suggested without politics and culture in mind. Navigating politics thus requires you to consider political relationships. Who can lend your idea powerful support? What group or individual has the organizational power to help or hinder your project? Whose ego might be threatened by your success? How can you win over powerful support in an ethical way? With whom do you need to chat over a cup of coffee in order to assuage their concerns or anxieties about change? Whom do you need to keep informed for reasons of power rather than reasons of truly needing to know? What old grudges or tensions do you need to skillfully resolve so that someone's ego does not motivate them to sabotage your project? What group or team do you need to support so you can win their support in exchange? How can you compromise with someone who opposes you? There are ethical and unethical answers to all of the above questions. If you carefully consider each question in consultation with others, you will be able to navigate the power relationships in your organization.

See beyond titles and org charts. Titles and org charts are useful, but they never tell the real story. Organizational awareness includes the ability to see beyond the official version of who is in charge. It involves seeing who actually solves problems, gives support, gets things done, provides leadership, builds teams, inspires action, and so on. Think of it as a parallel "invisible" organization that is more real and functional than the org charge version. Observing and understanding *that* organization is key to effectiveness.

Monitor the emotional economy. Listen to the buzz. Stay connected. What are people saying at lunch, at the coffee machine, and *after* meetings? What are the complaints? What are people excited about? Positive emotions are an organizational asset. Poor morale drains motivation, slows innovation, complicates change initiatives, and increases passive-aggressive behavior. Ignoring the emotional patterns of your organization is dangerous.

Examine and track inconsistencies. What's different between stated values and what *actually* gets rewarded and punished? If you are in leadership, you can be sure that many employees are noticing inconsistencies. At worst, such inconsistencies are interpreted as hypocrisy and can hurt credibility. At best, they are seen as part of an evolving process in an organization wherein leaders are aware, candid, and working toward fairness and effectiveness.

Scrutinize and discuss with others your organization's leadership. Examine strengths, weaknesses, style, and responsiveness to constituencies. Write a one-paragraph summary of key leaders' management style. Do you or your organization tolerate or even reward mediocre leadership? Is leadership style discussed? Discuss and give feedback about leadership style to raise the organizational awareness of the other leaders with whom you work.

Build social networks. Seek out new connections within your organization, not necessarily deep bonds. Keep the image of a spider web in mind when trying to be effective in leadership. Direct connections are more powerful than impersonal knowledge. You can positively influence the politics and the emotional economy of your organization if you carefully consider who needs to be invited to this or that event. Who needs to be consulted (sometimes for reasons of politics or network building rather than your real desire for a certain person's opinion)? Touch base with someone every day. Bring other people together who have something to offer each other. Acknowledge and celebrate a team or department's success. All these actions are investments in the human talent and the emotional economy of the organization. And they help you influence politics through positive social means rather than the stereotypical aggressive notion of politics.

LANGUAGE

♦ "Let's see if there's a trend here we're not noticing."

♦ "I know how the org chart says we should get this done, but let's be candid about some of the challenges our official setup won't adequately address."

- "I've noticed a bothersome trend in our organization, and I'd like to see if you see it, too."
- "I wonder how our leadership is viewed inside the company?"
- "Okay, let's get honest about the politics of the situation."
- "What's the buzz in the cafeteria? How do people feel about the changes?"

SELF-TALK

- *Who or what is really driving this initiative?*
- *Are the words I'm being told about the organization's values matching the actions I see around me?*
- *I need to stay connected. Keep networking.*
- *I can reach beyond my department to build a network.*
- *I need to listen and learn about the entire organization.*
- *What are the emotional implications of what I am telling my people?*
- *What are the politics of this situation?*

Part Four:
People Skills

14. Lead With Over-The-Horizon Thinking

Visionary leadership:
The ability to motivate others
with an inspirational vision and a
sense of shared purpose.

"Leaders keep their eyes on the horizon,
not just on the bottom line."
—Warren Bennis

"I was part of a company with an opportunity to be an early player in broadband communication. We had to choose between a quick profit or taking time to create something bigger. We knew we could build something more success-ful—and more exciting—if we were visionary. Why not take part in creating a new industry? All we really wanted to do was change the world!

"We started with team and leadership development of a group of engineers, product managers, and executives. We created a safe environment where we could exchange ideas, challenge each other to systems-thinking, and fast-forward ten years into the future. What would this new industry look like? What values, principles, and strategies would we have to embrace *today* to realize this distant picture?

"We also had to challenge the board to think beyond quarterly results to a five-year horizon. Engaging the hearts and minds of investors and potential customers was the most important early goal. When someone wanted to "do the numbers," we talked vision. Everyone involved ex-panded their thinking along with us, and saw that our idea had to be global to succeed. The board gave us the time to build a foundation for our vision. They supported small, nurturing steps. Eventually we got impressive financial re-wards, but only because of our visionary leadership."

Enhancing Visionary Leadership

Of the six styles of leadership described in *Primal Leadership* by Daniel Goleman, research found this style to have the most positive impact on the emotional economy of an organization. Visionary leaders motivate people to commit, to work hard, and to aim higher. They provide focus and inspiration. They help people feel and act "in synch." They acknowledge accomplishments and setbacks in a way that rallies productive energy. Such leadership helps drive performance. It also benefits the leader. When you have a clear vision and attend to your own need for positive emotions and clear direction, you create a buffer against your own discouragement. You gain energy from working for a purpose higher than profit. And you attract other positive-minded, visionary people to support you in your leadership.

ATTITUDES

♦ People need focus.

♦ People need their leaders to see far and clearly.

♦ A clear vision is good for the emotional economy of the organization.

♦ We are working for money, but we are also working for a common purpose.

♦ Leaders need to feel good about the direction the organization is moving. Others need that feeling, too.

ACTIONS

Get real. Visionary leadership is NOT synonymous with charismatic speaking. There *are* charismatic visionaries—and there are soft-spoken ones. True visionary leadership does not depend on personality or hype. It's about seeing further, evoking inspiration, and lifting up others. There are visionaries who inspire through humor or down-to-earth expressions, and others who quote Shakespeare. While you may benefit from improving your speaking and writing, you nonetheless have to find the visionary leader within. Then you must bring that part of yourself forward, rather than trying to fit a template. You have to be yourself or you won't inspire anyone.

Be clear about your own purpose. You cannot articulate a vision that is incongruent with your personal beliefs. You can't *fake* the role of visionary leader. To inspire others, you must first do the work of building your own personal foundation. You must love your career. And you must love leadership. You are most likely to get clear about your own values, goals, and vision through dialogue with others. If you haven't done this, get started.

Create a vision for your organization.[19] Obviously, the visionary leader must have a vision. It has to be clear in your own mind, and you have to have clear language for articulating it to others. You do not have to create it single-handedly. In discussions and correspondence, work with other leaders and thinkers to see where your organization can go. Look far enough ahead that your vision simulates wonder and motivation, but not so far ahead that you evoke disbelief or cynicism. A vision must inspire, but not sound absurd. The vision should motivate, focus, help people connect, inspire commitment, and point to results.

Keep it simple. An organization may be involved in extremely complicated technology or complex service activities, but the vision of what you as an organization can become should be simple. People remember and are stirred by simple ideas. They need to come up for air, so to speak, from the many complexities of their work and their personal lives. A vision is like a jolt of electricity that jumpstarts positive emotion. No matter how multifaceted the organization or what it creates, keep the vision simple.

Make it a picture they can hold in their minds. A vision should literally be a vision. Most people can hold an unpretentious picture in their minds—and feel positive emotion about it—more readily than they can respond to a memory of fancy words. When creating your vision, look for metaphors and images that people can easily hold on to.

Make it affirmative. Make sure your visionary language affirms rather than negates. Don't aim to conquer a disease; aim rather to free patients to live the lives they want. Use words like "more" and "better" and "greater" rather than their negative opposites.

Know your constituents. Your vision must not simply be your own. You must know your constituents: members of the organization, their families, customers, and others who will interact with you or be affected by your vision. You must find a vision and corresponding language that resonates with the people you want to inspire—from the executive to the knowledge worker to the hourly. You must create a vision that can become *their* vision.

Evoke emotion. A cold intellectual vision without the power to stimulate emotion is not very useful. *Motivation* comes from the same Latin root as *emotion.* Create a vision and a language that fuels the imaginations and the emotions of the people you lead.

Tap the power of values. You cannot evoke emotion if you do not know what your constituents value. What do they feel is important in life and work? What are they passionate about? What do they talk about and work for? The answers to these questions will help point you toward a vision that has profound meaning to your constituents.

Repeat it often. Most leaders who do have a vision do not repeat it enough. People need frequent reminders of where they are going. For the sake of variety and mental stimulation, you need more than one way to express the vision, but do not dilute it with too many clever phrases or metaphors. Once you find a few closely related ways to articulate your vision, say it often—in speeches, in meetings, and in one-on-one conversations.

Recruit other visionaries. As you build your organization or respond to change, try to get other visionary leaders to work with you. This is not about internal competition. You want a group of people who can think and talk in visionary terms, and collaborate from a shared vision. A well-orchestrated team of visionary leaders is an awesome force.

Develop person-to-person visionary leadership. In addition to the big vision you repeatedly articulate to many people, develop the ability to speak in visionary terms to individuals. When you're talking to someone about a promotion, describe where you see her in five years. Meet with a team to talk about their full potential and how to realize it. Inspire young leaders by describing a vision of what they can accomplish over a lifetime of leadership. Visionary leaders use their abilities in many situations—not to falsely inflate, but rather to tap the power of imagination.

Ask others about their vision. Just as there is motivational power in articulating your vision, it is powerful to ask others about theirs. They may not know what to say at first. In that case, you've stimulated someone to think forward. Or they may have plenty to say. Then you listen, thus sending the message that you are interested in their visionary thinking. In either case, you will be inspiring and motivating. That's visionary leadership.

LANGUAGE

♦ "Look how far we have come—*and* we're facing some huge challenges. But I think we're capable of . . ."

♦ "Let me tell you where I see you ten years from now."

♦ "We can reach much higher than this."

♦ "I'll tell you what I think this team can really do."

♦ "I believe we have a common purpose . . ."

SELF-TALK

♦ *People don't work only for money. They need purpose and direction, and I can help create that as a leader.*

♦ *Leadership is partly about inspiration.*

♦ *My role as a leader is to marshal positive emotions.*

♦ *How can I inspire this team?*

♦ *What can I say that will bring this company together with a shared purpose?*

♦ *Who can help me craft a powerful vision?*

15. Serve From A Mixed Menu of Persuasion Skills

Influence:

The ability to use a variety of persuasive methods to create "buy in."

"The only thing a title can buy is a little time—either to increase your level of influence with others or to erase it."

—John C. Maxwell

To watch Lee with a group of business people, you wouldn't pick her out as a particularly influential leader— not at first. But if you observe her over time, you see someone with a quiet but effective ability to influence others.

How does she do it?

She's rarely the first to speak. She often reminds people of what they've done that was successful or courageous. She speaks of "we" and "us" and the community, making people feel part of something. She takes time to chat with people when business is *not* being done. She offers her ideas as something to consider, rather than "right."

"When I have influence," Lee says, "it's because there's an issue I'm passionate about. And I'm passionate about a lot of things. I care deeply for my church and my kid's school, and I want my business to succeed. But I'm not always knowledgeable on subjects I'm passionate about. Over the years I've worked hard at *not* having opinions when I'm uninformed.

"When I work with a group of people, I first want to learn about them. I listen for their life experiences and their strengths. I try to find the best piece of each person. If I'm able to influence anyone, I think it's because they know I value them. If they believe I value their knowledge and ideas, they'll be open to mine as well."

Enhancing Influence

The Latin root of the word influence means "to flow." It implies that one is less likely to influence someone by force or manipulation that by working *with*. Whether you are in leadership, sales, a member of a technical team, or self-employed, you will influence others most effectively by developing a relationship—by connecting. Within the context of that relationship you can practice various methods of persuasion (e.g. logic, appeal to values, humor, etc.). Over time, you are more likely to influence others if they also believe they can influence you. A career, an organization—and a well-balanced life—are all best supported by a two-way flow of open minds.

ATTITUDES

♦ To be influential, I have to be "influence-able."

♦ If I want others to open their minds to me, I have to have an open mind.

♦ Connection usually works better than commanding.

♦ Different people are persuaded in different ways.

♦ Collaboration involves a two-way flow of influence.

ACTIONS

Practice "Connective Leadership." A universal principle of influence is *connection*. To connect with someone is to engage with that person emotionally, to find a common wavelength of meaning, to complete a person-to-person circuit. When people feel connected, important psychological needs get satisfied. When important psychological needs get satisfied, a person is more likely to cooperate, to try something, and to "flow" with you toward a shared goal. How can you connect with someone (and what psychological need will get satisfied)? There are many ways to connect. A shared *purpose* satisfies the human need for commitment. A shared *vision* helps meet their psychological need for inspiration and direction. A well-articulated *mission statement* addresses the need for clear goals. Office parties and get-togethers offer *affiliation*; people need to feel attached and cared about. When you connect with someone by *seeking input*, it fills the need for participation. *Empathy* joins people by meeting their need to feel understood. People feel linked through *humor* because we have a need to laugh and enjoy life. *Curiosity* connects people through gratifying the need for mental stimulation. When you practice these various ways of connecting with people, and when you get others to connect with each other, you are creating the conditions for higher motivation and a way of influencing that is not forced or resisted. People tend to be more motivated by connective leaders than by commanders.

Adapt to various personality types. You work in a diverse environment. There are many different personalities who must work together. To be effective, you must learn how influencing Person "A" calls for a different approach than Person "B". Trying to influence an introvert is often different than trying to influence an extrovert. You can learn through intuition or formal study when to influence someone through logic or when to use, say, a personal appeal. Adapting to different personality types starts with the idea that they are not wrong or "less than" for having a different personality that yours. From there, experiment with ways of having a positive influence. One style does not fit all.

Waste time and influence people. Detached or impersonal attempts to influence are generally less effective than something more personal. This means taking time to listen, to chat, to ask questions, to inquire about someone's life or their goals, to understand the other person's perspective and needs—this can be time well spent. It may seem like you're wasting time at the vending machine asking a colleague about her son's basketball game. In fact, such a conversation is likely to be time *invested* rather than wasted.

Affirm. No matter how old you are, you have a kid inside of you. If I try to influence you without affirming something about you, it's as if I don't see you. It's as if I don't value you fully. Simple affirming statements (that are not mere flattery) increase the probability of influencing someone. "You did a great job."

Communicate upcoming changes. Organizations are always changing. In leadership, you are frequently called upon to influence constituents to accept or cooperate with a change initiative. When people feel blindsided, they resist change. They become harder to influence. Instead of "buy in" you get opposition. Discussing changes before they are actually implemented gives people time to deal with their emotions. It helps them adapt and adjust. It makes it much easier to influence others.

Ask; don't tell. Sometimes you have to give orders. Sometimes you have to "be the boss." But with today's workforce, commanding others is likely to create resistance rather than buy in. It negatively affects morale. At worst it contributes to sabotage or high turnover. In contrast, anyone who works for someone they respect and to whom they feel connected is likely to attempt to cooperate when asked. People want to be influenced, not bossed.

Express curiosity about what others want. Everyone is self-motivated. If you want to influence someone, get to know what he or she wants. A person can be more or less persuaded by appeals to altruism, financial goals, ego, affiliation needs, family considerations, etc. Focusing too much on what *you* want from the interaction can miss the point and leave you unable to influence the other person.

Obey the law of exchange. If information or favors or support flow only one way, the relationship will be very limited. Just as nations and companies constantly trade, so do individuals and teams. When you attempt to influence someone, you are essentially asking for something. What will you give in exchange? What's in it for them?

Decide whether to be direct or indirect. In general, it is better to be clear and direct when trying to influence someone. Nonetheless, there are times when offering a hint or a suggestion plants an idea in someone's mind. The influence you are trying to achieve may be more powerful if that idea grows and blooms in the other person's mind, rather than being pre-packaged and delivered in a direct manner. Sometimes directness elicits defensiveness, while being indirect elicits reflection.

Logic can influence or backfire. There are some personality types who place the highest value on facts and logic. You will have no influence on such people unless you offer logical reasons for everything. Other people need a more values-oriented approach, or a passionate appeal. To rely solely on logic backfires with some people because they resent what feels like a completely impersonal interaction. It pays to think ahead and thoughtfully estimate the value of logic as a persuasive tool in any given situation. Most often you will be more influential with a combination of logic and other methods.[20]

LANGUAGE

♦ "I've got something I want you to consider."

♦ "I've noticed how hard you've worked lately."

♦ "I've noticed you have a real talent for working with the younger engineers."

♦ "What would make this more rewarding for you?"

♦ "I'm curious about what ideas *you* have."

♦ "Let's talk about some of the changes we'll be initiating in a few weeks."

♦ "This means a lot to me. I hope we can find a way for it to work for both of us."

SELF-TALK

♦ *How can I connect with him?*

♦ *How can I make this meaningful for her?*

♦ *Even though we're just chatting, I'm building a connection that will help me influence him.*

♦ *Am I open to being influenced?*

♦ *How can I bring out the best in this person?*

16. Apply R&D Thinking To Human Talent

Developing others:

Encouraging others' growth
through feedback and coaching.

"One does not 'manage' people. The task is to lead
people. And the goal is to make productive the specific
strengths and knowledge of each individual."

—Peter Drucker

Dennis has been developing people in retail for 25 years.

"My goal is to help sales people think like business owners." He focuses on career success for the individual *and* business success for the company. "Our firm is huge; it's easy to feel distant from the CEO. But every salesperson is the CEO of his or her own career. I think of my people as small companies interacting with a very large one."

His approach to mentoring is simple. "First I get acquainted. Even casual conversations around the drinking fountain help. Many sales people already have strong people skills, so I'm listening more for how they *think* about business." Then he follows their sales and looks for opportunities to give feedback.

"In the beginning I affirm *every* decision. I come back later to coach them on decisions that didn't go well. I don't tell them what they should have done, but we examine options that might have worked better."

Dennis wants sales that favor the customer, the business, and the sales associate.

"We talk about the cost of a sale, such as an extra service that closes the deal. What was the real business outcome of that sale? Did everyone benefit?"

Over time he develops confidence and thinking skills in others, which moves careers forward.

Enhancing Developing Others

Most jobs are more complicated than they were a generation ago. Organizations are becoming much more dependent on teams and collaboration to get things done. Leadership has become more complex as the workplace has become more diverse. All of these changes make it more important than ever for leaders and organizations to nurture and develop talent. Not to mention the fact that today's workers are looking for opportunities to develop themselves. Many professionals will accept a job that will help them develop their talent over one that pays more but neglects development. Developing others is a farsighted competency that invests in the future of an organization and its people.

ATTITUDES

- Develop talent or talent will go where it can develop.
- A good coach develops the bench.
- Helping people grow promotes innovation.
- The worth of an organization is partly measured in the quality of its talent.
- Developing others makes everyone smarter.

ACTIONS

Hire for emotional intelligence. Some people are easier to coach and develop than others. During a hiring or assignment process, you will certainly consider technical abilities. But also consider the competencies in this book. Which candidate is more likely to grow into an even more effective worker or leader? Think of emotional intelligence as a platform upon which you can build many other skills.

Give feedback. Feedback is gold to an individual's personal and professional development. It is also gold to an organization. Yet many people avoid giving it or receiving it. When it is given, it's often in a harsh or critical way. Or with no connection established first. Valuable feedback comes in two forms:

1) Reinforcing comments: Telling people they are doing something effectively and of value.

2) Adjusting comments: Telling people they are doing something that is not very valuable or effective, and guiding them on how to improve.

Examples of skillful feedback:

♦ "I overheard what you said to that customer about the delivery delay. You listened and took him seriously even though he was angry. That was a skillful way to save the sale."

♦ "I liked the beginning and the middle of your speech, but your last few comments were too detailed for this audience. May I make some suggestions?"

Ask people where they want to go. People are more motivated to engage in development activities if they believe it will further their individual interests. Asking people where they want to see themselves in three to five years gets their attention and stimulates thinking. Make it more than casual conversation, though. Take notes, ask follow-up questions, and stay connected. This is the first spark of a *real* personal development plan.

Remind people what they said about where they want to go. As time goes by, remind people of their goals. Show someone the connection between the challenging task you've delegated to her and what skill she said she wanted to develop. Make frequent connections between people's motivational goals and what you ask of them.

Push people. There's an obnoxious way to do this that creates resentment and backlash. But there is also an effective way to do it through which people accept challenge and stress because they know you believe in them. Most people rise to a challenge if they trust and feel connected to the leader who is pushing them. If you "push" with encouraging language and an eye on the individual's long-term development, you are more likely to ignite inspiration.

Affirm risk taking. If risk-taking produced only positive results, it is by definition not really risk-taking. If you want your team members or employees to create new opportunities and foster innovation, risk-taking is necessary. Affirm reasonable risks—including ones that don't produce great results.

Practice the 5-step coaching process: [21]

1. Create a clear goal statement. ("I like to see you become more assertive.")

2. Specify what behaviors demonstrate the skill. ("Express your opinions at meetings. Share problem solving ideas with the team.")

3. Express optimism to the change candidate. ("I think you can do this.")

4. Give qualitative and quantitative feedback. ("I like how you spoke up at the meeting. Twice you gave opinions that made the group look deeper into the situation.")

5. Praise loudly; complain softly. (Verbal affirmations motivate; embarrassment de-motivates.)

Discuss strengths and weakness in context. Most so-called strengths and weaknesses are contextual rather than absolute. The gregarious team member can get a difficult discussion going, but that same extroversion can be a weakness when the job calls for quiet reflection. When you offer feedback on someone's behavior, discuss various situations in which that behavior is an advantage and other situations in which it may serve as a disadvantage. This approach builds confidence and reduces defensiveness.

Use the "Sandwich Technique." Say something positive. Then describe what could improve. End with another affirming statement. This makes people more likely to get the meat of what you're telling them.

Set people up for success. When delegating or collaborating with someone, set the stage for a positive outcome. This is especially true early in a person's career. You want to build confidence early and work your way up to tougher, riskier assignments.

Thank people. Your grandmother probably told you this many times, and she probably didn't run an organization any larger than a family. But you can apply her words to an organization of any size. There are many short ways to thank people for their effort, skill, overtime, cooperation, favors, inspiration, kindness, ideas, and many other contributions to the organization. Grandma was right that saying "thank you" is good manners. It's also good business because it helps develop people.

Practice peer-coaching. Formal coaching or mentoring are valuable, but not always available. Forging an informal coaching partnership with a side-by-side colleague offers frequent "real time" opportunities for feedback, suggestions, and support.

LANGUAGE

♦ "Thanks for helping me with that. You did a great job."

♦ "I really liked the way you handled that situation."

♦ "Can I give you some feedback now? Or would you rather wait and talk this afternoon?"

♦ "I really like how you ran the meeting. You didn't let the group wander from topic to topic, but I think everybody felt like they had a chance to give their opinion. Good work."

♦ "There's a better way to handle stubborn employees. Let's talk about it."

♦ "You've got a talent for getting a team excited. But sometimes your humor makes people uncomfortable."

♦ "I'm going to push you to take this challenging assignment. I know it will add some stress, but I think you can do it and I know it will take you to a new skill level."

SELF-TALK

♦ *I can't just think about how my people are doing today. I've got to think how I can develop them for tomorrow.*

♦ *How can I set a tone for ongoing development so it is part of the culture of my organization?*

♦ *How can I develop this person's talent?*

17. Send & Receive On Several Wavelengths

Communication:

Knowing how and when to listen,
and the ability to convey ideas
with clarity and importance.

"Drowning in data, yet starved of information."

—Ruth Stanat

"I once took a philosophy book with me on a business trip to Japan. Somewhere between a Tokyo factory and ancient Greece I had an 'aha!' experience," says Hal, an engineer and executive.

"Like Japanese management, Socrates taught people to go beyond reflexively solving problems. He taught them to *think*. He did it through the art of asking questions.

"In engineering, you focus on the problem at hand. But after years in leadership, I knew I was overusing this get-to-the-solution thinking. Whether dealing with faulty software, customer complaints, or team emotions, I gathered data and jumped to recommendations. But I wasn't getting the best outcomes. Not with people. People are more complicated than machines.

"So I started practicing the art of the question. I cultivated curiosity when dealing with problems—whether they were human problems or technological. I slowed down, asked more clarifying questions. At first it felt like I was wasting time. Eventually, I realized I was *investing* time.

"The payoff? Fewer false starts and wrong turns. More valuable information. Improved collaboration with people whose problems I'm trying to solve. Better team thinking. Less wasted time and talent. Better results."

Enhancing Communication

All business deals, partnerships, and effective team accomplishments start and end with good communication. What you say and how you say it—and certainly how well you *listen*—has a major impact on how you and your organization perform. Communication is a bridge across the gap between you and others. At its easiest, you have to send clear signals over that gap. At its most challenging, you have to send complicated intellectual and emotional messages across a wide chasm of meaning. And that chasm is made wider by cultural, gender, and personality differences. Knowing what to say, what *not* to say, and how to receive what others are saying, has a powerful effect on progress toward your goals.

ATTITUDES

♦ Leadership begins with listening.

♦ Words have power. Non-verbal messages have power.

♦ What I *don't* say can be as important as what I *do* say.

♦ A little extra time spent on clear communication can save a lot of time, money, and stress.

ACTIONS

Listen.[22] It sounds so easy—but it's not. Nearly everyone can stand to improve their listening. Leaders do their best when they are great listeners. Below are several specific tips for improved listening.

♦ **Give your full attention to the speaker.** When someone is talking to you, giving the person your full attention sends the message you value the person *and* the message. Good leaders discipline themselves to stop what they are doing and focus 100% of their attention on understanding what the other person is saying.

♦ **Clarify.** Even careful listeners misunderstand some aspect of what a speaker is trying to say. The easiest way to make sure you "got it" is simply to ask some clarifying questions. It also lets the speaker know you are fully engaged.

♦ **Seek input and ask questions.** Strong communicators know how to get others to communicate. People are more likely to give input freely if they believe it is desired and valued. Smart leaders inspire others to contribute ideas and opinions by asking for them and listening to them. Great listeners know that people do not normally talk in complete, well-polished thoughts. Most people begin with the part that interests them most and then expand their thoughts into relevant side issues. Effective listeners show curiosity; they ask questions to help the speaker "flesh out" the message.

Pay attention to timing when expressing your opinions. If you are in leadership, you need to state your opinions clearly. Be conscious, however, of *how* and *when*. If you always speak first, you discourage others from speaking. If you express yourself too forcefully, some members will think your mind is already made up. If you use tact and timing, there is a much better chance that you will influence others with your opinions.

Explain the reasoning behind your opinions. Smart leaders explain their reasoning for the team to analyze and build upon. When you do this, your opinion is more likely to win thoughtful consideration. You also set an example for others to do the same.

Ask others for the reasoning behind their opinions. Helping others explain their thinking gets them more involved in the discussion and encourages them to evaluate their own conclusions. Take care not to discredit or dismiss opinions. Try to probe in a non-threatening way for the facts and assumptions behind opinions.

Avoid point-counterpoint debates. We hire attorneys because they are masters of debate. They are trained to win a legal contest. But most of the activity inside a team or organization is not a contest. Team objectives will not be reached if the leader simply debates the members. Debate can be a powerful and useful tool for some jobs. But it can be the wrong tool for the job when dealing with team conflicts, creativity, or personal relationship difficulties.

Put away "cooperation killers." There are many phrases that unintentionally zap team spirit. For example: "I know what I'm talking about." Or "I can't believe you really think that." Many leaders also use sarcasm to cope with stress and conflict. They might get a laugh at the expense of teamwork. And non-verbal expressions such as eye rolling or looking at your computer screen while someone is talking can send strong anti-collaboration messages. This may all seem obvious, but when we are exposed to stress, discouragement, or hostility, we sometimes have a subconscious impulse to push people away or lash out. Leaders must be able to control their emotions and consciously choose effective verbal and non-verbal messages—even when others do not.

Study someone who has a reputation for being a strong communicator. Select a role model and observe that person for choice of words, facial expressions, body language, and tone of voice. Let that person influence how you communicate. The goal is not to mimic, of course, but rather to take some aspects of someone else's effective communication and incorporate it into a style of your own.

Avoid communication waste. Time is a valuable resource. Keep most voice mails to 30 seconds. Make most emails only a few lines long. Start and end meetings on time, and follow an agenda. There are exceptions to these guidelines, for sure. But for the most part—short is sweet.

Consider the medium. Email is good for sending documents and quick messages, but bad for conflict resolution. Telephone is good for discussion, but your voice has to make up for unseen facial expressions. Face-to-face is best for negotiation and difficult discussions.

Be clear about the purpose of any speech, meeting, or discussion. Communication is clearest and most productive if people know *why* they are communicating. Are we making a decision? Are we simply exploring possibilities? Are we trying to solve a problem? Let people know the purpose of a discussion or written communication.

Stick to one or two points. Don't overcomplicate a discussion or "flood" people with information. People can only receive so much. It is better to cover a few points per meeting, discussion, or memo. Have a specific message you want to send, say it clearly, and then let others take it in.

Sometimes indirect is better. While clarity and to-the-point communication is generally effective, sometimes it is not. There are situations in which hints or understated comments are more likely to be heard than the plain truth. "Your public speaking abilities are weak" may evoke a motivation to improve, or simply elicit defensiveness. "I think some members of the audience were restless" may not get the point across, or it may "save face" and stimulate self-improvement. Consider the person and the situation when deciding how direct or indirect you need to be.

LANGUAGE

- "Let me see if I understand. Are you saying _____?"
- "Let's spend some time making sure we understand each other."
- "Here's my main point . . ."
- "Let me explain my reasoning."
- "I have some questions for you. The reason I want to ask you these questions is _____ . . ."
- "You're quiet today. I'd like to hear what you're thinking about this."
- "Let's explore the issue now, and decide Monday."

SELF-TALK

- *Don't shoot the messenger.*
- *How can I tune my message so it's clear?*
- *Have I really listened to others' perspectives?*
- *I need to choose my words carefully here.*

18. Spark An Evolution

Stimulating change:

Initiating and/or supporting innovation,

leading people on a new path,

and willingly facing obstacles.

"If you create an atmosphere of freedom where people

aren't afraid someone will steal their ideas,

they engage with each other. They help one another."

—Robert Redford

"This is a story of a brilliant R&D scientist and a wise manufacturing engineer," explains an executive for a high tech firm. "The goal of product development is to create something manufacturing-friendly. R&D invents a draft but often gets tired of it by the time manufacturing has to get the bugs out. Success depends on working together through the launch. Well, the scientist has lots of talent *and* a big ego. So the engineer has to handle him skillfully.

"Let's say there are three processes for a new product. The scientist is responsible for Process A. Then he gives it to manufacturing, and the engineer has to make B and C work. But there may be problems in all three. When the scientist sees problems, he quickly announces to the engineer, 'I know I got *my* part right. Take a look at B and C.'

"The engineer doesn't argue. 'Okay. I'll run some tests.' He comes back with data and says to the scientist, 'Can you help me figure this out?' The scientist says, 'Sure, I can help you.' But when the scientist looks at the results, he sees problems in his own area. He's got to look closer and work with others to find solutions.

"Innovation is as much a human process as a technical one. The engineer's official job is to make products better, and he does. But he also makes people better. And by doing that, he makes us a better company."

Enhancing Change & Innovation

Innovation drives progress—and profit. It can be techno-logical innovation or new approaches to problem-solving, new ways to motivate people, or new services. Change can be good, but it's scary; it disrupts organizations and stresses people. Furthermore, misguided or mismanaged change creates resistance. Change introduced for the sake of a leader's ego—rather than added value—hurts motivation. Many entrepreneurs impulsively leap into change, then flop. Many managers introduce change without enough communication only to create new problems. Many innovators ignore the need for collaboration, and watch their great idea die. However, when change and innovation are guided by emotional intelligence, they are more likely to be effective and sustainable. Stimulating innovation and leading people in a new direction takes creativity, courage, wisdom, and communication. The payoff? An organization that demonstrates these same competencies and reaches its goals instead of stirring up resistance.

ATTITUDES

♦ Part of my job as leader is to create excitement and encourage curiosity.

♦ Every obstacle is a challenge to be overcome.

- Change for the sake of change is inefficient; change for the sake of real improvement is progress.
- Sometimes survival demands that we change.
- People execute changes better if they help create them.
- There's probably a better way to do what we're doing.
- Innovation requires collaboration.

ACTIONS

Articulate a clear vision of the future.[23] Teams and organizations need a challenge. A clearly stated vision produces a drive for improvement and innovation. It provides a context for change. It makes change feel less arbitrary, and thus reduces anxiety and resistance. Remember JFK's speech about reaching the moon in a decade? That vision stimulated innovation.

Frequently ask for ideas and suggestions. If you are serious about soliciting ideas, you need to make the process easy and satisfying. People have to believe their input is really wanted and will receive serious consideration. That means asking for suggestions, giving them balanced evaluation and ensuring that the right people are involved.

Suspend criticism until ideas have been heard and explored. Research shows that when teams feel free to offer all sorts of ideas—rather than just *good* ideas—they generate *more* good suggestions than teams that try to submit *only* good ideas. It is important to separate *generating* ideas from *judging* ideas. Do not let brainstorming degenerate into a debate about the pros and cons of something.

Commit time and other resources to supporting promising new ideas. To survive, a good idea needs to be supported in many ways. Time must be given for people to work on it. Tools, equipment and materials must be committed for its development. It also needs intangible support like creative input and encouragement. Leaders must combine good judgment with imagination to decide when and how to support a potentially promising idea. Are you really supporting the ideas you say are promising?

React constructively to challenges and setbacks. Experienced leaders expect problems and obstacles to arise in the face of innovation. The key is to react to problems quickly and pragmatically, rather than getting stuck in blame or negativity. Change agents focus on solution-oriented thinking. Leaders need to help others understand the problems and obstacles, devise ways to overcome them, and do so in a way that keeps them focused on the task at hand in a constructive frame of mind.

Give praise or recognition to people who work on innovative projects. It is hard to work on a project with uncertain outcomes and frustrating obstacles. People who take risks and invest energy need to feel rewarded for their effort. Leaders need to recognize *everyone* who contributes—people who offer ideas, people who devote time, and the "champions" who bring ideas to fulfillment.

Never kill a new idea. The initial value of an idea is not how well it will ultimately work, but how much it supports continued creative thinking. Value every idea in its germinal form. Very often a creative but impractical idea eventually leads to a new product or procedure that is extremely pragmatic and profitable. If you kill a new idea, you're killing its descendants as well.

Delete "killer phrases" from your vocabulary; they block innovative thinking. Killing off an idea is as easy as not watering a seed. Avoid knee-jerk comments:

♦ "It's a good idea, but..."
♦ "That's not our problem."
♦ "The old way works just fine."

Make brainstorming sessions a habit. Identify topics about which you and your team can take 5-10 minutes to brainstorm a list of ideas, questions, problems, solutions or alternatives. The basic rules are:

♦ Anyone can offer an idea.
♦ No criticism.

♦ Record them for all to see. It's easy to do and a great way to pool ideas.

♦ Distinguish the critical analysis phase of the discussion from the brainstorming phase.

Remember that "champion" is a verb. To champion an idea or new approach is to protect it, promote it, support it, stand up for it, and take some heat. "To champion" is an action verb. It requires courage, stamina, and vision. Every step forward in an organization or society was championed in the face of opposition before being widely accepted.

Express and encourage curiosity. Curiosity may have killed the cat, but it's good for organizations. That's not to say it's always welcome. People get comfortably set in their ways and curiosity challenges them to think new thoughts. It can be discomforting. But it's also stimulating, and leads to better solutions as well as innovative products and services. If you are in leadership, openly and frequently express curiosity. When you hear someone else express curiosity, reward them with your interest and with supportive comments (even if their curiosity does not lead anywhere productive in a specific meeting). Think about creating a *culture* of curiosity rather than insisting that every expression of curiosity produces results. Encourage your innovators to engage with each other and collaborate.

Question common sense. Common sense can be non-sense. It used to be common sense that . . .

♦ The world was flat.

♦ "Made in Japan" meant poor quality.

♦ Women and minorities can't succeed in leadership.

Of course, common sense can also make sense (e.g. "practice makes perfect"). To be an effective change catalyst, you need to practice distinguishing between common sense and common fallacy.

Recognize need for change. Change agents keep an eye open for what can improve. They analyze systems for what is wrong, inefficient, or unfair. They develop the habit of looking at things from several angles, and imagining progress. They don't just think *new* thoughts; they try to frequently think *pragmatic* new thoughts.

Create "buy in" for changes. Not everyone is a curious innovator or a change agent. Simply announcing or imposing organizational changes can create massive resistance, and thus backfire. Attend to the change *process* if you want important changes to succeed. Some crucial aspects of the change process include:

♦ **Focus on the early adapters.** Many leaders put too much energy into converting the strongest resistors, rather than creating buy in with an influential group of people whose resistance is minimal or zero. If you get enough influential and open-minded people to buy into the changes, some of the resistors will follow. There will always be a small percentage of people who will resist change no matter what.

♦ **Seek input.** Through focus groups, surveys, and informal discussions, get the people you lead to talk about changes they want to see, or how they feel about upcoming changes. There are two benefits to this: First, you are probably not a genius and have probably overlooked something. The janitor, the department manger, the technician, the secretary—all have a perspective on things that will help you make better decisions. Second, if they feel that you value their input, they are less likely to resist change even if it isn't the change they prefer.

♦ **Communicate about and explain upcoming changes.** Most people do not like surprises at work. If people have advanced notice of coming changes, and some reasonable explanation for *why* the changes are coming, they have time to adjust their expectations and emotions. And they have time to make decisions that give them a much-needed sense of control. Many leaders do not understand this. Insufficient communication is a major reason some change initiatives fail or create expensive resistance.

LANGUAGE

♦ "Why do we do it this way?"

♦ "I like that idea. Let's play with it."

♦ "Is there a new way to think about this situation?"

♦ "Remember, we're brainstorming. Every idea, no matter how crazy, can be part of this discussion. We'll do some reality testing later. Let's think creatively, folks."

♦ "Let's come up with a communication plan so our people have advance notice of these changes."

♦ "Let's try to understand the resistance to these changes."

♦ "I'd like to explain *why* we're changing things."

♦ "I'm curious about your reactions to these changes in the company."

SELF-TALK

♦ *I need to listen to this new idea. It doesn't sound very realistic now, but maybe it will lead somewhere.*

♦ *How can I challenge the mindset of this meeting?*

♦ *How can I recognize the risks this person took to innovate and find new solutions?*

♦ *I need to listen to this perspective on the upcoming changes in the organization, and not dismiss it.*

19. Practice Navigating In A Storm

Conflict management:

The ability to de-intensify conflicts
and coordinate workable solutions.

You can't shake hands with a clenched fist.
—Indira Gandhi

Jim was new to the position of Division Director in a U.S. Government lab. His boss was asking how he would handle the revolt against Tom, a Branch Chief who "as of today is *your* headache."

Jim started with questions. He learned that Tom had met with the ten scientists who reported to him—only to bark at them. They barked back. Jim decided to discuss the situation with every person involved. He got an earful of rage.

He learned the most from Tom himself. After hearing many complaints about other scientists and the job itself, Jim probed Tom about his interests. Tom had an understated passion for science, as well as two kids in college.

"I asked for this job," he said. "But now my research is stalled." Eventually Tom realized he wanted less management duty. A promotion that kept him from work he loved was no promotion at all. He returned to research.

Over the next year, Jim rotated different scientists through the Branch Chief position. The conflicts decreased as the group gained respect for the job. The fourth person in the job was good at it and settled in.

Jim's advice about conflict: "Listen and ask questions first. And at the end of the day, put the right people in the right places."

Enhancing Conflict Management

Conflict is a necessary and valuable aspect of teams and organizations. If there are no "storms," it is a sign of people withholding valuable feedback or new ideas. But conflict is not always productive. Workplace anger—and sadly even violence—can hurt people, discredit leadership, and increase turnover. The ability to encourage *productive* conflict on teams and within partnerships, while at the same time reducing or preventing *destructive* conflict, involves skills that bring tangible and intangible benefits to an organization. The intangibles—a safe environment, creative tension, honest feedback, positive emotion, and more—are inherently humane and make your organization an attractive place to work or do business. The tangibles—productive teams, innovation, lower turnover—are good for the balance sheet as well as sustainable high performance.

ATTITUDES

♦ Some forms of conflict are good for an organization, even if they make people uncomfortable.

♦ Some forms of conflict are highly destructive to an organization.

♦ As a leader, avoiding conflict is not an option.

♦ There are positive ways to manage conflict.

ACTIONS

Understand the distinction between *productive* conflict and *destructive* conflict.[24]

♦ **Productive conflict:** Examples include debate, disagreement, creative tension, team "storming." These forms of conflict may make people uncomfortable, but they help move the organization forward.

♦ **Destructive conflict:** Examples include hostile language, harassment or coercion, violence, threats, harsh criticism. These forms of conflict are uncomfortable to talk about, and so often get avoided or overlooked.

As obvious as this productive/destructive distinction may appear, many people are anxious about conflict in general, and will avoid talking about either form of conflict. Furthermore, in their early stages, the two forms are more likely to be confused. If your colleague has a life history of being harshly criticized, your well-intended challenging remark about the marketing plan may unintentionally induce anxiety to the point that your colleague does not offer her valuable thoughts in return. The creative process shuts down. An emotionally intelligent leader has keen eyes and ears for both forms of conflict. Such a leader knows that the presence of destructive conflict is extremely damaging to an organization, *and* that the absence of productive conflict hurts as well.

Create a climate of zero tolerance for destructive conflict. It takes more than well-written policies to eliminate destructive conflict. It takes leadership grounded in emotional intelligence, collaboration, and assertiveness. Such leadership responds quickly and firmly to any form of destructive conflict, and creates a climate wherein people are not afraid to report it. Such leadership knows that such a response makes moral and practical sense. This does not mean that an employee is instantly fired for minor offenses such as a hostile remark. But it does mean that destructive conflict is addressed in its early forms whenever possible. A combination of the competencies described in this book is brought into play to educate and mediate with the relevant parties—before the conflict grows into something major. And when the conflict is already at a high level, the emotionally intelligent supervisor or manager takes whatever courageous action is necessary to protect individuals, groups, and the organization. This includes the willingness to enter into productive conflict with higher levels of authority in the organization.

Create a climate that encourages productive conflict. Some leaders, in an attempt to discourage destructive conflict, try to create a general climate of "harmony" and in the process discourage *all* conflict. But the team that appears to have no conflicts is an underperforming team at best. And it isn't without conflict anyway. Because conflict is natural in human relationships, such a team has covert conflict disguised as harmony. A highly effective team has open conflict that is well managed. The team leader and members use emotional intelligence competencies to work through their conflicts, find compromises, explore and test each other's ideas, and innovate—rather than avoid conflict and pretend they have no differences. To create a climate where such productive conflict is encouraged and well managed, keep these principles in mind:

- **Conflict is inevitable.** It is based on the natural fact that people are different. There are differences of personality, opinion, gender, cultural background, and more.

- **Put it on the table.** Open conflict is more productive than indirect or covert conflict. It takes good listening, good facilitation, and emotional control to bring conflict into the open. If you don't bring conflict out, it will either subvert the creativity and effectiveness of the group, or will come out later in a destructive form.

- **Go beyond "winning."** The concept of winning applies to some conflicts. In sports, war, elections, and gambling, the concept works fine. But the most positive outcome of a productive conflict at work is not "winning"—it is creativity and effectiveness. As a leader, you will often be dealing with people who get stuck in the concept of winning. Help them get unstuck by emphasizing teamwork, shared goals, and "win-win" outcomes.

Allow for emotion. Conflict brings up strong emotions, especially anger and anxiety. Don't shut these down in yourself or others. As long as they are not expressed with hostility, they are part of the process of conflict management. At the same time, some individuals deal with conflict stoically. Don't expect or require everyone in the situation to emote. Allow emotion, but don't require it.

To deal directly with conflict:

♦ Observe team members. Stay connected and informed.

♦ Find time to talk to members privately. Explore each perspective on situations that may create disagreement.

♦ In a team meeting, openly acknowledge conflict.

♦ Create a relaxed, trusting environment and facilitate discussions that bring out all points of view.

♦ Clarify where there is common ground and where there are clear differences.

♦ Remind team members of the team's purpose and goals.

♦ Ask the team to bridge the gaps in perspective: "How can *we* accomplish our goals given these conflicts?" "Where do individuals need to compromise or be patient in order to achieve the larger goals of our team?"

LANGUAGE

♦ "It sounds like everybody is in agreement, even though we've only briefly discussed this. I have a hunch that some members of the team have other perspectives."

♦ "Sam, I'm trying to respect your point of view, but I cannot tolerate the hostility and your threatening tone."

♦ "I know there's a lot of tension in the team right now. There is some sort of conflict occurring that is not being expressed. Let's get more honest and talk about what we are avoiding."

SELF-TALK

♦ *Although I feel uncomfortable with this conflict, I know I need to stay engaged in this discussion.*

♦ *This is a productive conflict. It's good for the team.*

♦ *This conflict is not productive; I need to take strong action to protect individuals and the organization.*

♦ *If someone resorts to hostility to make a point, I need to interrupt and provide assertive feedback.*

♦ *I need to keep listening for common ground and a possible win-win solution.*

20. Weave A People Web

Relationship building:

A knack for developing and maintaining
an array of productive relationships.

"No matter what accomplishments you make,
somebody helped you."
—Althea Gibson

"We build enduring relationships."

That may seem like an odd mission statement for a law firm, but one of its partners, Kyle, claims it's as important as knowing the law.

"We are competent lawyers," he says. "But to build a thriving practice in a town *full* of competent lawyers, you need more than that. We're not just selling legal expertise; we're selling trust, and connection, and peace of mind. Those come from steady relationship building."

Internally, the partners build enduring relationships with each other, day by day. "We've come to trust each other through a lot of honest conversations and commitment. We keep on talking even when we strongly disagree."

Outwardly, Kyle's focus is also on relationship building. "I make a few calls a day just to let someone know of a relevant opportunity or an idea. If I were obsessed with the concept of billable hours, I wouldn't make those calls. Because I do, I have all the business I want."

"We also build relationships with other professionals in the area. Doctors, accountants, etc. But we go beyond simply passing along business leads. We get to know some of them very well, and we become advocates for each other."

Enhancing Relationship Building

At the end of the movie *It's A Wonderful Life*, the main character realizes he has built so many strong bonds in his life that he will never be allowed to fail. In organizational life or in business for yourself it is much the same. Strong personal and professional bonds provide motivated allies when you face setbacks. They also strengthen you when you face a challenging frontier. They provide a context that encourages candor when you need another perspective. And they enhance your quality of life by fostering social connection, teamwork, and celebration of success. Such bonds are built the way most people build their bank account, through small but frequent day-to-day activity rather than dramatic get-rich-quick schemes. The gradual accumulation of getting to know someone, exchanging knowledge, working together effectively and supportively—add up over time to create a wealth of commitment and productivity.

ATTITUDES

♦ Getting to know my coworkers has an indirect but powerful effect on the work.

♦ It's practical to ask others about their family, their dreams, and their ideas.

♦ I build bonds and improve teamwork when I listen well.

- How can I get the people involved in this project to connect with each other more?

- Building relationships creates a more productive organization.

ACTIONS

Learn about personality types. You don't have to be a shrink to gain some useful knowledge about individual differences. Obviously there are many different types of people, and understating something about type is analogous to speaking many languages. You can learn how to get through to different people in different situations. If you only speak one "language," you can effectively bond with only one type of person. There are several systems for sorting people into types. A trip to the library, an Internet search, or a conversation with someone who already has a knowledge base can educate you quickly. You don't need to be an expert.

Understand that "small talk" can have a big payoff. "Small talk" sounds wasteful to highly productive people—like it's unrelated to reaching goals. But a measured amount helps get things done. Asking people about their kids or aging parents takes a few minutes but makes a meaningful deposit in the emotional bank account. Such small actions over time accumulate good will and greater motivation. And they build bonds.

Have a connecting conversation. This goes deeper than small talk. It involves questions like, "What do you want out of life?" and "What are your big career goals?" It can entail topics such as marriage or losing a loved one. Some people crave such conversations and feel very connected through them. These talks can have a fruitful effect on work relationships. But some people experience them as very uncomfortable. If you understand the type of person with whom you are talking, you can gauge whether such a talk will bond you or separate you.

Touch base. Phoning a colleague or customer when it's not really necessary can nonetheless be practical. Nowadays many people work with others around the region, nation, or world. Staying connected by voicemail, email, or "touch base conversations" keeps the bonds strong and ensures that when you really need to work closely with that person, you are not starting from scratch.

Exchange favors. Some people are just not that interested in talking. And some people who do like to talk are also very action-oriented and build bonds through giving and receiving favors. To do for others, especially when someone is under stress or a time crunch, is not only a good example of the Golden Rule, but it also creates connection.

Tangible actions are the best way to build productive bonds with some people.

Don't get lost in the age-old introvert-extrovert contest. Each personality type has its strength, and its own effective way of building bonds. If you're extroverted, it's easier for you to start the process of connecting with someone. If you're introverted, don't worry. You have your own way of taking steps to turn a stranger into a collaborative partner. The point is to know how you do it, polish your skills, and start building. It helps to make a list of things you've done in the past to build useful bonds.

Play golf (or don't play golf). Think about golf. Of all the sports, it involves the least amount of exercise, especially if you use a cart. But golfers enjoy fresh air together, stroll, talk, and take a break from highly focused work. Half the purpose of golf is to build bonds. If you don't like golf, don't fake it. Focus more on the importance of building bonds and look for other activities that accomplish the same thing.

Smile. Trite but true. Walking into your office in the morning *without* a smile discourages people from interacting with you. Even a one-second exchange of "good morning" helps build bonds. A simple smile actually makes a small but significant daily deposit that adds up over time.

Follow-through. For highly task-oriented people, words mean nothing without action. To build a meaningful and productive bond with such a person, you must follow-through on promises, not matter how busy you are. If you promise more than you can deliver, your intention will mean less than your broken promise. In addition to the fact that important work may not get done, you will be straining a bond rather than forging one.

Make it fun. Some individuals are most likely to connect with others and produce better results when there is fun involved. This does not refer to any sort of immature or inappropriate fun. But when there is room for laughter, friendly competition, or other ways to make demanding work feel lighter, most people feel more connected and thus are more motivated.

Give gifts. Simple, thoughtful ones. A birthday card. Memorabilia. An article the other person will find interesting. It's not about the financial value of the gift; it's about letting the other person know you pay attention. It's an investment that pays off in positive emotion and productivity.

Have team social events. If you are part of a team, building group bonds can be achieved by getting out of the office together. Celebrating success and friendship through parties, celebrations, and holiday gatherings—all have a purpose that helps work relationships and improves quality of life.

LANGUAGE

- "I know you're in a crunch; what can I do to help?"
- "How did your son do in the tournament?"
- "Let's think of a way to make this project more fun."
- "I'm calling just to touch base. How have you been?"
- "I'm calling because I heard about an opportunity today that you might be interested in."
- "Let's get the team together outside of work—just to relax and catch up with each other."
- "Let's do lunch."

SELF-TALK

- *I don't have to be great friends with this person, but it would be helpful to have a connected work relationship.*
- *All I have to do to get started is to ask a question.*
- *I'm not as extroverted as him, but I still have ways of building productive bonds.*
- *What would be the best way to stay in touch with this person, given her personality type?*
- *How can I help my team bond so we can function best and enjoy our work more?*

21. Set Sail On Strong Partnerships

Teamwork and collaboration:
An aptitude for establishing a climate
of cooperation and solidarity.

"Talent wins games, but teamwork
and intelligence wins championships."
—Michael Jordon

"One of our devices had a problem that was hard to diagnose. Same problem from a year earlier. We thought we had fixed it, but the problem came back. It was part of a complex supply chain, so we took the device apart and contacted each supplier. 'It's not *my* fault,' each one said.

"There was just no collaborative spirit.

"I studied the history of the problem. Bob, our former Chief Engineer who had tackled the problem a year earlier, was autocratic. Instead of guiding suppliers to a deeper analysis of the problem, he told them what to do.

"When I talked to suppliers the second time around, they weren't invested in Bob's solution. But they *were* willing to do pretty much anything I told them to do. 'Just tell us what you want us to do,' one said in a conference call. I said: 'I don't know what I want you to do. I just know the result I need. You're the experts on your products. I need all of you to work with my team of engineers to solve this problem once and for all.'

"Many meetings and many experiments later, we found a solution that stuck. The problem was too complex for one person—or even several people in the same company—to solve. It took a team of strong personalities to come up with new ideas—and to test them without much defensiveness."

Enhancing Teamwork & Collaboration

The products, services, and problems of today's organizations are too complex for solo efforts. Nearly every project takes a cooperative effort. You may be technically brilliant, but without the ability to collaborate your gifts will be largely wasted. Teamwork and collaboration are thus basic ingredients in any effective organization. Furthermore, it's quite likely that some aspect of getting your work done depends on interacting with some very different people—different cultural backgrounds, different personalities, different value systems. It is one thing to collaborate with someone just like you; it is more difficult (and more valuable) to team up with someone different than you. Leveraging diversity requires emotional intelligence. And as if all that were not challenging enough, the world of organizations is only going to get more complex, more highly structured, and more diverse. The future belongs to emotionally intelligent teams and collaborative leaders.

ATTITUDES

♦   If you have a dream, you need a team.

♦   Collaboration is how to leverage talent.

♦   Collaboration is how to leverage diversity.

♦   To build a team, you have to build trust.

♦   None of us is as smart as all of us.

- It is more effective to delegate and collaborate than to dictate and intimidate.

- People are not part of the organization. People *are* the organization.

ACTIONS

Clarify the purpose of the team.[25] A team is not just a group of people who feel good working together. An effective team has a common purpose that members can state clearly. In addition to being able to clearly state the purpose, the team's actions demonstrate that purpose every day.

Define specific goals and measure progress. More specific than purpose, a team needs clear goals that members work toward and measure progress. People invest more of themselves in teamwork when they are aware of specific, measurable goals. Measurable goals also motivate team members to think creatively about problems and setbacks. There are two levels of measurement; both are important.

- **Process measurement:** How often you *try* a new skill. ("You tried twice as many 3-point shots today as you did in the last game. You're getting more confident.")

- **Outcome measurement:** How often you *achieve* the ultimate goal. ("You scored 12 points from the 3-point range. That helped us win.")

Share leadership. A high functioning team may have an identified leader, but that leader is no autocrat. Such a leader knows the power of *sharing* authority—and supports decisions made by the team. To frequently veto team decisions sends the signal that the leader does not trust the team's judgment, which breeds resentment and cynicism. By consulting with the team, the leader helps members feel ownership in decisions. People give input if they believe it is desired and valued. Smart leaders inspire team members to contribute ideas and opinions by asking, listening, and giving credit where credit is due.

Make roles clear. Make sure people have a clear idea of what their contribution and responsibilities are in a situation. Collaboration makes people interdependent. Lack of clear roles affects everyone—and the bottom line.

Learn to interact with different personalities. Teams are typically made up of very different people. This makes it challenging to understand, communicate and work together. If you can learn to appreciate and trust team members who are different from you, you can build high-performing teams based on each member's strengths.

Deal with conflict directly. Collaboration can create disagreement and friction. Treating such conflicts as bad can lead people to hide information and avoid each other.

Without skilled leadership that helps navigate conflict, a partnership or team or organization never realizes its potential for creativity, effectiveness, and collaboration. When there is conflict, start with listening, of course. Try to diffuse strong emotion. Diffusing emotion does not mean squashing it. Let people vent some, and ask them to explain their frustration or anger. Empathize with their perspective even if you disagree with it. At some point you many need to say, "I understand there is strong emotion about this, but let's stay focused as a team and talk about how we can move forward." Try to shift the concept of "blame" to the concept of "responsibility." These are different. Blame invites guilt and attack. Responsibility invites analysis, learning, and problem solving.

Communicate effectively with your team. Keep these communication tips in mind:

♦ **Start with listening.** Always. Otherwise you set up a debate format, or you unwittingly encourage people not to talk candidly. This can kill team spirit and effectiveness. *Always* start with listening.

♦ **When you don't know something, admit it.** Don't let ego or embarrassment derail the team. The team's IQ is cumulative. No single member has to be a know-it-all.

- **Don't discount any idea out of hand.** Give individuals and the team a chance to float ideas. The collective thinking of the team, as well as good data, will sort out the practical ideas from the impractical.

- **Ask questions.** Get data. "Hmm. Tell me how that idea evolved. Have you tested any aspect of this idea?" Don't respond too quickly to the reply, or the team will stop answering your questions frankly. Use this phrase, "That's interesting, let's think through this together."

Discuss the technical and political history of a problem or project. Sometimes a team is set up to repeat mistakes made in the past. Hence it's important for members to understand the history. Are there politics or personalities that could derail an otherwise good solution? Are there technical or systemic barriers that have not been understood? If previous individuals or teams failed at the same endeavor, ask "Why?" Smart teams ask themselves, "What do we have to do differently to succeed?"

Represent the team effectively to the organization. No team works in a vacuum. Make sure the rest of the organization has current information about team projects. If team members believe they are being misrepresented or undervalued by the organization, trust and morale will suffer.

Praise collaborative effort and results whenever warranted. Give credit and recognition only when it is earned. When you give praise, be specific about what aspects of someone's work mattered most. For example: "I want to thank you for staying late last night to fix that program. Your willingness to jump in made the difference."

Use a carrot rather than a stick. When people are threatened, they think about survival, not creativity. Team members who are worried about negative ramifications for making mistakes will just try to get by. When you are trying to motivate a team, attraction works better than aversion.

Ask team members what the barriers are to better teamwork. Have a brainstorming session to answer the question, "What is standing in our way of becoming a better performing team?" List responses on a flipchart and have the team rank them from most important to least. Ask them to identify what *you* might be doing that is a barrier to better teamwork. Say something like, "If there is something I am doing or not doing which you think is getting in the way, feel free to let me know." When team members begin to tell you what you are doing wrong or what you are neglecting, do not explain yourself. Keep listening and thank them for the feedback. You can evaluate it later.

Improve the fit between people and assignments. To get maximum contribution from everyone, good leaders delegate projects and decisions based on the strengths of individual team members. Consider these criteria when making assignments:

- Does the person's skills fit the need?
- Does the person want the assignment?
- Will the assignment help this person learn and develop?
- Will this assignment help develop an advantage for the team or the organization in the long run?

Help people learn from setbacks. There is no better teacher than experience and no better learning opportunity than a mistake. Effective leaders turn setbacks into learning experiences by collaborating with people to:

- Review what happened . . .
- Analyze the causes . . .
- Consider alternative approaches . . .

To continuously improve, have "lessons learned" discussions on a regular basis. Periodically ask colleagues, "What lessons can we learn from this situation or from this problem? What worked and what didn't work? How could we do it better next time?"

LANGUAGE

- "I want us to work on this together."

- "Let's think about whose strengths match this task."
- "What can I do as the team leader to better support or guide the team?"
- Let's review, for clarity, the purpose and roles of this team. Let's keep that in the front of our minds."
- "Let's deal with this conflict. Let's meet as a team and get things out in the open so we can work together."
- "Please speak up if you disagree with how we are approaching this project. It's our job as a team to help each other prevent mistakes."
- "You did an awesome job putting the numbers together for the team report. That was a huge help."
- "The fact is, this is a big setback. But it is also an opportunity to improve how we approach complicated problems. Let's look back and learn from whatever mistakes we made."

SELF-TALK

- *I need to listen and clarify first.*
- *In the short run we'd be better off if I solved this problem myself. In the long run we'll be stronger as a team and an organization if we solve it together.*
- *I think I see the best course of action right now. But if I speak first, I may prevent the team from doing the work of finding a solution that's as good or better.*

A Vision of you as Leader

Think back to your first leadership experience. No, not your first job with an organization. Further back. Think about high school or earlier. You were on a team, or part of a club, or were playing a game with some friends.

You were probably bossy, sulky, or you begged to get your way. Primitive leadership skills. Maybe your were effective, maybe you weren't. But that's where leadership starts.

Look how far you've come. If you are at the beginning of your leadership career, look at how much more finesse you have. You can sometimes get people to work together. You can collaborate. You can influence others. If you've been at this a long time, you probably have some leadership experiences you feel very good about. You already have strengths in emotional intelligence.

Now look at how much more you can still develop. Organizations are complex and ever changing. The workforce is evolving. The world economy is changing. Leadership skills are not static. Different organizations and different times will demand different things of you.

You've got years and many opportunities to increase your effectiveness even more, and to adapt to new situations. As you continue to enhance your emotional intelligence, imagine yourself achieving important career goals. Imagine contributing more to a company, a school, a church, a community. Imagine helping others develop—so that your leadership abilities have a rippling effect. However gifted (or clumsy) you are at leadership, whatever your strengths and weaknesses, you'll look back five years from now and feel proud that you continued to grow.

Notes

[1] This book focuses on techniques and strategies for enhancing emotional intelligence, rather than theory and research. For a thorough study of the theory and research related to emotional intelligence, we recommend the books of Daniel Goleman, especially *Emotional Intelligence: Why It Can Matter More Than IQ*. We also highly recommend publications produced by The Consortium for Research on Emotional Intelligence in Organizations (www.eiconsortium.org).

[2] *Working with Emotional Intelligence*, by Daniel Goleman (Chapter 1).

[3] Ibid., Chapter 3

[4] *Primal Leadership* by Daniel Goleman. Different authors and researchers have offered various classification systems for the many competencies of emotional intelligence. We have used the classification system of Goleman because it is most widely known and so well thought out.

[5] For an excellent model of team effectiveness and emotional intelligence, see *Building the Emotional Intelligence of Groups* by Venessa Urch Druskat and Steven B. Wolf, available through Harvard Business Review (www.hbr.org).

[6] This list is based on information provided in *Working with Emotional Intelligence*, by Daniel Goleman, as well as our extensive experience working with individuals in organizations.

[7] For additional information on benefits to organizations, see *The Emotionally Intelligent Workplace: How to Select for, Measure, and Improve Emotional Intelligence in Individuals, Groups, and Organizations* by Cary Cherniss (Editor), Daniel Goleman (Editor).

[8] This technique is basically a do-it-yourself 360° assessment. We recommend that anyone serious about developing his or her leadership ability participate in a 360° feedback periodically. Getting the assessments of others helps develop accurate self-assessment.

[9] For a well-written treatment of this idea, we recommend *There's No Such Thing As "Business" Ethics: There's Only One Rule For Making Decisions* by John Maxwell.

[10] Often a lack of conscientiousness comes from not having a disciplined system for time management and other productivity techniques. If you need more help than this book offers, look into the books and CD's of David Allen, such as *Getting Things Done*, and *Ready For Anything*.

[11] For in-depth self-help on increasing assertiveness, we recommend *The Assertiveness Workbook: How to Express Your Ideas and Stand Up for Yourself at Work and in Relationships* by Randy J. Paterson PhD.

[12] *Do What You Love, The Money Will Follow: Discovering Your Right Livelihood* by Marsha Sinetar.

[13] For additional information on resilience, see *Managing Change With Resilience* by Linda Hoopes & Mark Kelly, and *Managing At the Speed of Change* by Daryl Conner.

[14] *The 7 Habits of Highly Effective People* by Stephen Covey.

[15] Some of the techniques in this chapter are summarized from *Learned Optimism* by Martin Seligman.

[16] The three types of empathy are summarized from *Emotions Revealed: Recognizing Faces and Feelings to Improve Communication and Emotional Life* by Paul Ekman.

[17] For more "How To" information on empathy, we recommend *Lifeskills* by Redford & Virginia Williams.

[18] To study the topic of organizational culture further, consider the books of Edgar Schein, such as *Organizational Culture and Leadership* and *The Corporate Culture Survival Guide*.

[19] One of the best books addressing visionary leadership is *On Becoming A Leader* by Warren Bennis. You'll see why it's a classic. We also highly recommend Goleman's treatment of this topic in *Primal Leadership*.

[20] For more information on influence, we recommend *Artful Persuasion: How to Command Attention, Change Minds, and Influence People* by Harry Mills.

[21] For more on coaching, see *Mastering Team Leadership: 7 Essential Coaching Skills* by Kelly, Ferguson, and Alwon. Also *Masterful Coaching* by Robert Hargrove.

[22] For a reference book on the broad topic of communication, consider *Excellence in Business Communication* by John Thill, and Courtland L. Bovee. We also recommend *Harvard Business Review of Effective Communication* by Ralph Nichols.

[23] For more on leading change, read *Leading Change* by John P. Kotter.

[24] A good "How To" book on this topic is *Managing Disagreement Constructively: Conflict Management in Organizations* by Herbert Kindler.

[25] For some great books about teamwork and collaboration, we recommend the following:
- *The Five Dysfunctions of a Team* by Patrick Lencioni
- *The Wisdom of Teams* by Jon Katzenbach
- *Mastering Team Leadership: 7 Essential Coaching Skills* by Kelly, Ferguson, and Alwon
- *The 17 Essential Qualities of a Team Player* by John C. Maxwell.

Meet the Writing Team

ROBERT FERGUSON is a psychologist, executive coach, and leadership trainer. He is an associate at Raleigh Consulting Group, Inc.

Contact him at
Ferguson@RaleighConsulting.com

MARK KELLY is a management consultant, executive coach, and leadership trainer. He is a partner at Raleigh Consulting Group, Inc. This is his sixth book.

Contact him at
Kelly@RaleighConsulting.com

Photographer: Victoria Kelly

Printed in the United States
67303LVS00003B/577-600

9 780970 460622